MW00466628

Tracks

Tracks

Donald C. Jackson

University Press of Mississippi / Jackson

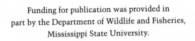

Funding for publication was provided in
part by the Department of Wildlife and Fisheries,
Mississippi State University.

www.upress.state.ms.us

Designed by Todd Lape

The University Press of Mississippi is a member of the
Association of American University Presses.

First Edition 2006
∞

Library of Congress Cataloging-in-Publication Data
Jackson, Donald C., 1951–
Tracks / Donald C. Jackson.— 1st ed.
p. cm.
ISBN-13: 978-1-57806-894-4 (cloth : alk. paper)
ISBN-10: 1-57806-894-0 (cloth : alk. paper) 1. Hunting—Southern
States—Anecdotes. 2. Hunting—Alaska—Anecdotes. 3. Jackson,
Donald C., 1951– 4. Nature—Psychological aspects. I. Title.
SK43.J33 2006

799.2975—dc22   2006000136

British Library Cataloging-in-Publication Data available

Contents

Contents

Tracks

Wilderness Before Dawn

Most people who ramble around in the outdoors, hunting, fishing, or just tromping around, have conjured up images of themselves as explorers of remote mountain ranges, voyagers of the northern lake country, or perhaps fur trappers, deep in wilderness, alone with land, sky, and water. There is a sirens' call that makes folks like us restless to be off and gone . . . living on that bittersweet path of adventure, challenge, freedom, overwhelming beauty, and probably self-imposed poverty. We courageously "give it all up" in our minds, and dream of old cabins, worn rifles, wood stoves, curing meat, deep snows, and fresh tracks.

However, somewhere along the pilgrimage of most would-be wilderness wanderers, choices are made that preclude taking up the pack. We sense that there are so many wines to taste in life and so little time. So, professions are established. We get married and have families. Commitments are made to God, country, community, loved ones.

This is a fine trail, a path with a heart, and one that typically generates a deep sense of purpose and fulfillment. It's been the foundation for human civilizations for millennia. But, as fine as this trail may be, the sirens' call will not be stilled. It is always there, swirling around in our hearts, capturing our quiet moments, speaking of wilderness and the ways of the wild.

Some who hear the sirens' call to wilderness have opportunities to answer it. I surely have. As a professional in natural resources, I have had the good fortune to wander the earth, probing the hidden pockets of the wild places. I've traveled deep into the jungles of Asia and tropical America, camped alone for weeks in the deserts of Australia, climbed among the world's tallest mountains in Nepal, explored the forests across the face of North America, trekked across Arctic tundra, slogged through swamps and marshes of all sorts, and shared the African plains with wildebeast, antelope, buffalo, and Masai. Although I've experienced "the wild" in these ventures, the sense of true wilderness seemed always to elude me.

I thought perhaps that the missing element was hunting, so I took off in pursuit of big game. I shot elk in the Rocky Mountains, caribou, moose, and wolf in Alaska's arctic and another caribou out in western Alaska, bear in the rainforests of southeast Alaska, and deer all across the southern U.S. Some of the hunts were tough. Some were dangerous. All were wonderful ventures and are treasures wrapped up in my heart. But the sense of wilderness still wasn't within those big game hunts.

I turned to other game, particularly ducks, and went to some of the world's best spots. Whistling wings somehow beat in cadence with the sirens' call. The "wilderness" was closer, but still beyond my reach.

The basic problem was that I never really felt "alone." I never really felt that the rest of creation was moving and being as it should and would were human-kind less of a force in the world. There was always something: another hunter on a distant slope or shore, a muffled shot from another valley or ridge, the whine of an outboard somewhere on the river, lake, or bay, the smell of smoke drifting on the wind, the sound of distant tires on pavement or gravel, aircraft overhead. These were like knives disconnecting me from the soul of wilderness. I was unable to grasp the indescribable chill I'd experienced in my dreams, that icy thread that in wilderness courses from the earth through a human body and into the spirit of humankind.

I turned to fishing. There was solitude in the places I fished, and a good bit of the wild. But still those dis-connecting knives of human enterprise plagued me. Lakes and reservoirs were hopeless. They were plagued by noise and gamblers who demeaned the fish by mak-ing contests out of them. Ponds were better, particu-larly those tucked away on someone's "back forty," and streams were the best of all because their movement tended to drown distant noises. But streams carried their own sort of trash, the visual sort that was inescap-able. Footprints were the worst because they reflected short time between myself and an intruder. The cans and bottles were cancers, eating away at the life of my encounters, and the turbidity so characteristic of many streams these days reflected humankind's disrespect for the land.

I became desperate. There was nowhere to turn, no way to follow, no untrammeled pass. Finally, in resignation, I accepted a world without wilderness. I had to be content just with the wild. But there was a problem. The sirens still called.

"Where the heck are they calling from?" I asked myself in mounting frustration. "Surely there's still a place."

The answer to my question came not from some distant sojourn but rather from my own little farm that is about six miles from my home in Mississippi. My farm is just a trifle less than fifty acres and sits back off the main county road about half a mile. There's a bit of woods on it, some lowland and some on a hill. Typically these woods have good populations of grey squirrels and fox squirrels. A creek twists across one corner of the farm. There are two ponds, one wild and tucked back in the woods, the other larger and more in the open. Wild ducks and occasionally geese use them. Around the ponds and along the creek, the raccoons and opossums prowl.

About eighteen acres of the property are in pasture, but I've encouraged the edges to creep back into wild states. I have had quail in this area from time to time. In the extreme northwest corner of the property there's a quiet sector where deer drift out of the woods and into a small clearing at dusk. Each autumn I take two or three of them. My family rarely buys meat. Along the northeast edge, broom sedge dominates and provides a hangout for coyotes that sing to me in the evenings and sometimes at dawn. I've only seen one bobcat on the place, but grey fox are fairly common.

Although I'm fifty-four years old, I have a relatively young family. Aside from my work as a university professor, my days are full of all the other things a young family does. The day begins well before dawn for my wife and me, with exercises and runs to keep the tickers in shape. Then there is the mad rush to get the kids fed, properly dressed, and off to school. Afternoons and evenings are choked with a flurry of activities: soccer, scouts, gym, karate, ballet, music lessons. Weekends are for church, scout activities, haircuts, cutting grass, working in the garden, conducting projects on the farm and around the house, and running errands. All-day hunts of the sort that can still the soul of the restless man are out of the question. An hour or two on a deer stand in the occasional evening after work, or forty-five minutes a couple of mornings a week trying to catch the first flight of ducks over the pond are about all I can negotiate.

Subsequently, and over the years, the sirens' song grew pretty faint. I concentrated on my little farm, trying to do what I could as a wildlife and fisheries manager, manipulating the system, trying to help it be the best that it could be. But in spite of my efforts, quail declined on my farm, wood ducks became less and less productive, and persimmons disappeared prematurely from the tree near my stand where I bow hunt for deer.

I planted more and different sorts of food plots for the quail, and millet around the ponds for the ducks. I built more wood duck nest boxes, and made sure they were clean and fresh with new cedar shavings every year. I entered into an agreement with the U.S. Fish and Wildlife Service to expand my pasture pond to create more wetland habitat. I fertilized around the persimmon tree and cleared away competing saplings. I built brush piles and planted pines and hardwoods to create buffer zones and travel corridors.

My efforts really didn't seem to make any difference. The quail disappeared completely, and once I went an entire year without even *seeing*, much less shooting, a wood duck on my property. The persimmon tree was the picture of health and productivity, but the fruit seemed to disappear all the faster. Then I made another observation. All over the farm, the muddy spots, the stream banks, and the shallow areas around the ponds were full of "varmit" tracks. It dawned on me that I needed to become a trapper if balance was to be restored.

I had some traps I'd bought back during my rambling days, but they were still neatly packed in their original box. I'd purchased them one day when I was dreaming about an alternate path . . . a path that never materialized. I dragged out these traps from a dusty back corner of my storage shed and tried to figure out what to do with them. I'd read something about water sets being the way to go for raccoon and went about my affairs with that orientation. I got some wire and stakes and, after a little coaching by a local trapper, caught my first fur—a grizzled old "coon" down by my wild pond. The bug bit.

I discovered something beautiful and deeply fulfilling. I found that trapping is an art, and that a good trapper is typically an excellent woodsman. The trapper has to think like the critter and figure out just where the foot will step. I learned that you can manipulate an animal's steps through creating travel funnels and "step-over" logs. I found out that raccoons cannot pass by a hole in the ground, and especially one along a creek bank. They absolutely *must* put a paw in to check it out. A trap or two alongside, and a step or two from a hole can be deadly. I learned that you really shouldn't run your traps too early because you'll miss some hits, but that a man can run his line really early and not interfere with all the other stuff that a family and job require of him. This last reality prevailed and I got into the habit of running my trapline between 3:00 a.m. and 4:30 a.m. The freedom to ramble was precious.

One morning, while I was rambling around my farm checking my traps, breathing in the freshest of air, and listening, and looking, the unexpected happened. It was a cold morning. The moon hanging over my pond was so bright that it sparkled on the frost that covered my pasture. It was a magic morning, still and deep and a little bit spooky. I was walking slowly, carrying a couple of raccoons I'd taken from my traps. I could feel the heft of my "fur" pistol hanging from the belt on my hip, and the soft ground through the soles of my black rubber knee boots. Although it was cold, I was warm from my walk. There was a song in my heart. I felt so alive, so real, so in tune with God. An early morning walk can in itself be a prayer.

Then I heard sirens' voices drifting upward from my soul. Their songs surrounded me, filled me with energy, and set my heart on edge. I stopped and just stood there in the open, under the sky, with stars hanging like jewels just beyond my reach. Something stirred. It was like a wind but very deep, very internal. I felt a chill. I sensed a connection with the earth. The siren songs grew louder in the stillness. The stars shone and the moonlight made the pasture nearly as light as day. The shadows in the woods were sharp and distinct and mysterious.

I could hear the rustling of critters on leaves and in the grass. Sticks snapped in the shadows. A fox barked. A pack of coyotes tuned up. As I watched, deer melted in and out of the shadows by the pond. Something dark and low to the ground scurried across the pasture. Wild geese flew overhead unseen but full of gabble. Leopard frogs called from the wild pond back in the woods. The sirens' voices became a symphony.

There was no noise from traffic on the roads . . . it was still much too early. Overhead there were no aircraft, not even the high-flying commercial and military planes . . . still too early. There was no smoke from chimneys . . . too early. There were no gunshots . . . too early. It was still a couple of hours before the first train would pass through town about ten miles away. I heard nothing, saw nothing, felt nothing but the wild.

I was enveloped by the purest of elements in creation. I was alone, absolutely alone in a world very different from the "daylight world." The sirens' chorus sang, "Wilderness, wilderness, WILDERNESS!!"

The truth smashed into me with full force. The world at 3:00 a.m., even on a tiny Mississippi farm on the outskirts of a college town, was the very wilderness I'd been seeking. Wilderness has evolved from being a place into being a time. And within the context of time, wilderness has transformed its way, its nature, its very sense of being. It has relinquished its hold on the "day world" and now rules beyond boundaries during the night.

To be a part of wilderness, I have had to become a creature of the night. I have had to enter into the realm of the night winds, the rustling branches, the migrating geese, the calling frogs, the whip-poor-wills, the prowling predators, the monster whitetail bucks, the biggest fish, the longest snakes, the shadows, the reflections, the sparkles . . . the quiet.

The sirens still call to me, stronger than ever before. And I respond in full force to their call, capturing chunks of life in the wilderness when nobody else is calling my name. I may not be able to spend year upon year in the north woods running a trapline, but I surely can spend year upon year as a trapper under the stars in my own wilderness. Between midnight and 4:00 a.m., when the sky is so deep it seems to swallow the earth, the wilderness I prowl is alive, well, and kicking. And so now is this wilderness trapper.

And the trapping? Well, it *is* the catalyst that linked me to wilderness that special morning, and trapping continues to link me with it now. I suppose I could just ramble at night and not trap. But it wouldn't be the same. Part of the sirens' call to me is combined with old dreams and visions and songs of the wilderness wanderers of yesteryear, the voyagers, the explorers, the mountain men, the fur trappers. I'm not out there in the wilderness just to observe. I have to be a part of what's going on. The traps pull me from my home and into a frigid world just as they pulled the old fur trappers from their north woods cabins. I live by my efforts just as fur trappers have done through the ages . . . but the living I earn is not economic. I earn a living measured by fullness of heart, not fullness of pocketbook. I don't catch much and I don't sell what I catch. Some treasures aren't sold.

Carefully spread across the couch in my study are the tanned pelts of five prime raccoons I've taken from my farm. They are precious to me, reminding me as I write on this cold, wet February afternoon that the wilderness is just twelve hours away. I reach over, stroke them, pick one of them up, and smell its sweetness.

And I whisper to myself, "I'll be there."

To Kill a Bear

Hunters respond to primitive echoes. They recognize that within them swells a dimension which links them strongly to ages past. Although in their wilderness ramblings they may nurture themselves as naturalists, poets, or artists, the essential ingredient of their ventures centers around the confrontation between man and beast.

There comes a time for some hunters when those echoes drive them deep into the wilderness in pursuit of great carnivores. In North America that generally means bears. Regardless of the species, bears are tough, big, and perfectly capable of killing a man.

Back when I was living in Alaska, I faced the truth that as a hunter I had to kill a bear. It didn't come as a quick decision or during some moment of inspiration. Rather, it required deep deliberation.

Bears are not usually hunted as a source of meat even though the meat can be good and is often eaten. The killing of a bear, unless for defensive purposes, falls under other reasons which I had to think about for a long time.

I don't hunt for sport. Rather I hunt because there is an ancient urge within me which will not otherwise be addressed. Hunting is not fun. For me it runs deeper than that. Hunting is a response to an overwhelming calling and in hunting there is satisfaction and a confirmation of identity.

When my decision to kill a bear had been made, I was faced with deciding what bear to kill and where to do it. There are strict regulations governing the killing of bears. But it is possible for a determined hunter to kill any bear he wishes in North America. Decide what bear you want, then persist until you get him.

I decided to kill a big black bear. The black bear is the only bear in North America which is found exclusively in North America. I decided also that I wanted to kill my bear in Alaska. There were two reasons for this. Alaska is the wildest place that I personally know in North America and there are more black bears there than anywhere else on the continent.

My decision was confirmed late one afternoon when I was returning to Fairbanks from hunting ptarmigan with a friend of mine, Dean Rhine. We'd stopped at a roadside tavern for a beer and there, hanging on the wall, was a magnificent black bear hide. The fur was long, thick and, in the soft light, it glistened like black satin. I've been around a lot of bears and I've seen a lot of bear skins from a variety of species, but I'd never seen a more beautiful bear hide than this one there before me on the tavern wall.

Although my decision had been made, I found myself forced to leave Alaska before I could get a decent hunt organized. For two years I brooded and planned. My friend Dean, meanwhile, shot three black bears in southeast Alaska and kept sending me photographs and invitations. We planned a hunt for September 1987, but I was forced to cancel. I found that as important as bear hunting may be, it takes second priority relative to the responsibilities a man has to a young wife with a one-month-old son.

During the following winter Dean moved from southeast Alaska north to Valdez. I hunted small game and deer in the Deep South but my dreams were all about bears. Finally, unable to wait any longer, I called Dean one Sunday afternoon to see if he wanted to pull off a spring bear hunt. The answer was a strong affirmative and we started making plans.

I arrived in Alaska the last week in May. Home again in the land which owns my heart and soul, I felt my senses sharpen almost immediately as the plane touched down on the runway at Anchorage. My mind cleared as I focused on the hunt that lay ahead.

On the short flight from Anchorage to Valdez, it was obvious that winter still lingered on in the Prince William Sound area. Snow lay deep in the forests, with white fringes still stretching to the beaches in protected places. Icebergs jammed the passages between glaciers and many of the islands. Looking down upon the land, the water, the ice, and mountains, I knew that of all places on this earth, this place . . . this far northland . . . is where I belonged.

Dean met me at the airport, and we quickly outfitted ourselves with provisions enough for a week or two of hunting. I bought my licenses and a bear tag. Then off we went to the rifle range just outside Valdez to sight in our guns.

It was late evening by the time we set up at the range. There was a chill settling upon the land which put a sparkle in the air and stiffened my fingers. The musty smell of thawing Alaska penetrated my senses and etched itself anew in my mind. As we fired our rifles the echoes lingered among the mountains as if to announce our intentions to any and all who cared to take notice. But, between our volleys, only the ravens seemed to care. Only they joined us in breaking the late evening hush. Alaska is so overpowering that even the blasts of high-powered rifles are overwhelmed and smothered.

Alaska was all around me that evening and within me filled my heart nearly to the point of bursting. The strength of a man swells within him in Alaska. There is no restraint. Be what you are, who you are. Go where you will. Follow your dreams. With one hand touch the earth with all its grandeur and pulsations of life. With the other, reach out and touch the face of God. In Alaska there is no room for compromise.

Early the following morning we loaded Dean's boat with all our gear, provisions, and a borrowed canoe.

Slowly we cruised out of Valdez harbor in the misty, cool shadows of dawn, past sea otters and floating seaweed and on into the waters of Prince William Sound.

The world was ours as we skimmed across the slick water. Only the eagles and an occasional seal suggested that life was present beyond the boat. But we knew better. The forested slopes and open valleys that we passed are the best black bear country in the world. In fact, we were concerned that we might kill our bears on this, our first day of hunting, and deny ourselves the opportunity of first establishing a full state of communion, an intimacy, with the spirit of the land.

Eventually we were forced to slow down as we picked our way through the ice fields spawned by Columbia Glacier. Changing pace gave us a chance to catch up with ourselves . . . to settle down . . . to begin glassing the beaches and grassy slopes for black spots which could be bears.

All morning and most of the afternoon we hunted. Anchoring the boat, we launched the canoe and cruised silently along the protected shorelines of the north shore coves. No bears were spotted, nor did we see any sign. Eventually we beached the canoe and began climbing up into the higher spots where snow lingered. We crossed bear tracks but they seemed old and far too few. Only soaked boots resulted from these excursions.

Returning to the canoe, somewhat disillusioned, we sat on the beach and held a powwow. Had this area been hunted out? Should we push on farther or return to hunt the hill country around Valdez? I concentrated hard, wishing for a bear with all my might. Then, suddenly, across the bay, there appeared a black spot.

I grabbed my binoculars, and sure enough, that spot had four legs, a long neck, and a furry old head! The bear was at least a half a mile distant across the water. He looked like a decent bear, worthy of the effort required for a long paddle across open water and a careful stalk.

Bears depend on their senses of smell and hearing. Although we'd be pretty obvious out in the canoe, if we watched the wind and stayed quiet, chances were that we'd be able to get a crack at the bruin. Our plan was to paddle straight across the bay. This would take us out of sight of the bear. From there we'd drift quietly along the shore until we passed some rocks beyond which the bear was feeding on fresh grass. But, when we eventually got to where the bear was supposed to be, nothing remained but some cropped-off grass and some tracks on the hillside.

I tried slipping through the woods in hopes of a glimpse of the critter and a shot. But my efforts were to no avail. Black bears are just too sharp to put up with that sort of nonsense.

Returning to the canoe, my spirits were, however, high. At least we'd seen a bear. The bear had escaped but somehow that seemed good. I'd have killed it, given the chance, and then my half of the hunt would have been over. It was better this way.

Paddling back to the boat, we decided that the best thing for us to do was to move on farther down the coast. We'd search out a good anchorage for the night and resume our hunt the following morning.

During the process we spied one nice bear down near the water's edge, but he saw us almost immediately and was gone in a flash. Muscles rippling under his rich black fur, he tore across the slick rocks, jumped across a jumble of driftwood, and quickly melted into the green jungle of the Alaskan coastal forest. These beasts can move with amazing speed and given half a chance can reduce themselves to only memories in hunters' minds.

Both Dean and I were pretty well beat by the time we found a suitable spot to hole up for the night. Checking the navigation charts to be sure we wouldn't end up on rocks during low tide, we set anchor. Dean went to shore for fresh water, and I worked to get supper going onboard the boat.

Dean's boat would serve as our camp this first night out. The seats convert to beds and, with a tarp secured over the aft end of the cabin, we would be snug, dry, and out of the wind.

With supper washed down by a couple of cans of beer apiece, we crawled into our sleeping bags. My mind went spinning off into the never-never land. I was enraptured by the reality of being back in Alaska. The rocking of the boat and the sound of a gentle breeze drifting across the bay spoke deep messages to me.

The next morning Dean dropped me off in a small sheltered bay surrounded by mountains and with a couple of valleys stretching back to the northeast. Then he left for Valdez, approximately fifty to sixty miles away, to pick up a couple of friends of ours who wanted to hunt with us for a day or so. Plans were for him to try to return to camp sometime later that day, but provisions for a week were left with me. It was calm in the little bay but pretty rough out in Prince William Sound. He would risk the trip back only after conditions on the sound improved.

How I loved it . . . the silence, the loneliness, the grandeur of mountains, sea, and sky . . . moving from rocky beach to high ground, trip after trip, packing gear on my back and filling my soul with a deep song from my heart. Truly, I was home again. The air coming off the mountains sank into the nearby nameless valleys and slid down them, brushing my face—cooling me, whispering my name. "How could it be," said the whisper, "that you left this land? How is it that you will leave again?" I had no answer except that when I am away from Alaska, my heart and soul remain there.

I'd been shuttling gear for perhaps an hour when I looked through a break along the shore and spotted a black bear on a distant grassy beach. He was perhaps six hundred to seven hundred yards away. From my previous experiences with these bears I knew that this fellow wasn't going to spend much time exposed out on that beach.

So, grabbing my day pack, which contained extra ammunition and my camera, in one hand and my old .30-06 rifle and a paddle with the other hand, I slipped down out of sight to the beach below camp. Then I returned to the high ground, threw the canoe to my shoulders, and trotted down to where the rest of my gear lay on the beach.

Swiftly I loaded the canoe, pushed off, and paddled as silently and as quickly as I could along the opposite side of an isthmus which separated me from the bear. The strokes were strong and deliberate. My mind and body were absorbed with the mission of stalking that bear. Everything stood out in sharp contrast—the trees, the rocks, a patch of snow, the black speck of a raven along a cliff. From time to time I had to work my way across shallow spots, but the canoe allowed me to slip over the rocks with no sound.

Finally, I arrived at the back corner of the little bay and beached the canoe. A flock of goldeneye ducks flew up in front of me and whistled away on stiff wings. But, at this point, the ducks and I were still well hidden from the bear by a small rise covered by spruce trees.

I grabbed my rifle and day pack and slipped into the woods as silently as possible. It was wet and still among the trees. Thick moss carpeted the ground, old logs, and the lower portions of most tree trunks. I moved through this wonderland cautiously but knowing that time was the critical element if I were to catch that bear still out in the open. As I approached the edge of the woods, I stopped to scan up and down an open area I had to cross. I didn't want to accidently bump into that bear in a premature encounter, and I needed to get my directions straight.

There was no bear in sight.

Easing down onto the wet rocks, I began to stalk slowly toward where I thought the bear could be seen. As I did this, I glanced to my left and saw a big Canada goose watching me from some seventy yards away. Not willing to allow me to pass in peace, the goose started honking loudly and raising such a ruckus that I was sure the bear, if still around, would be spooked.

But I pressed on in the din, higher and farther toward some rocks that I figured would give me a pretty good view of the area where I'd first spotted the bear. The goose couldn't believe that I had the nerve to continue with my intrusion of its domain and went absolutely berserk. Finally, honking and complaining, it took to the air, filling the entire area with its loud cries but, fortunately, was soon far off and out of earshot.

I topped the rocks that had been my objective and there, across a tiny cove into which a small salmon stream flowed, stood the bear at the edge of the woods. He was busy eating leaves from some bushes and apparently had not been much bothered by the commotion caused by the goose.

A hush settled upon the scene. The water lay flat and mirror-like below the rocks. The air had an electric quality to it as the drama of an impending bushwhack began to take shape. The world shrank. Nothing existed except bear, man, and rifle.

Settling down into a prone position, I took a steady rest for my rifle on a rock. The bear was about 150 yards away. The wind hardly existed, but what tiny traces did were from the right direction—from bear to me. The ambush setup was perfect.

A calm settled over me. Being there was so right. The moment was magic. There was a confirmation of my deepest identity.

The bear moved out of the bushes for just a moment and the crosshairs of my rifle scope settled on his chest. At 4X power, I had a tremendous target—black, burly, muscles rippling under a glossy coat, jaws snapping and grinding away at the bushes. As the crosshairs settled, I let out half of my breath, steadied the rifle just a bit, and touched off the shot.

The bear was literally knocked off his feet by the impact of the 150 grain bullet. He rolled out of the bushes and was down on his back. I jacked another round into my rifle and held down on him again. Now, on his side, still kicking, he raised his head. I let him have two more quick rounds and he settled down. In no uncertain terms did I want the task of tracking a wounded bear through the thick, tangled forest beyond the beach.

Wild ducks, alarmed by my shooting, filled the sky with whistling wings and quacking. Seals splashed and slapped the water in the bay. Then my bear let out a long, trailing moan which reverberated hauntingly across the water and bounced off the faces of the surrounding mountains. The loneliness of it all—the primitive, chilling reality of killing this great beast—penetrated to the core of my being, touched me with a precious, beautiful sadness, and caused me to swell with the impact of participating in so basic and fundamental a drama.

If, somehow, our roles had been reversed and the bear the victor, I knew that in my last moments I would have felt this same sweetness. Somehow this bear and I had been joined by the spirit of primitive encounters which have echoed down through the ages.

Now, all was still. I had my bear on the ground. Sitting there on the rocks, I watched him for several minutes, just to be absolutely certain he was down for keeps. Then, slowly, I collected myself, two of the three spent brass cases lying on the rocks (I found the other one a day later), and my old camouflaged hunting hat, which had been knocked off my head by the blast of the first shot. Picking my way carefully along the slick rocks, I returned for the canoe and portaged it across an open, narrow spot of the isthmus separating the bay from the cove with my bear.

I paddled across the cove and beached the canoe on some rocks just below the bear. Then, checking my rifle, I slowly walked up to where he lay. From out in the cove the bear had been but a small black lump in the green grass. Now, close up, he was much larger than I had imagined. In fact, he was much, much larger than I'd ever hoped for.

With loaded rifle I approached him slowly and punched him in the ribs with the end of the barrel. There was no sign of life. I punched again—no stirring.

The bruin was dead.

Quickly I checked him over. There wasn't a rubbed spot on him. The hair was thick, deep, and glossy. Only a couple of scars on his face, one old, one new, in any way marred the beauty of this animal. As far as I was concerned those scars gave him character. This bear had been a scrapper.

After stretching him out and realizing how big he was, I wondered if I'd be able to handle him. He was well over six feet long from tip of nose to tip of tail, and, stretched out, his hind legs added a couple of more feet to that length. He was heavy—at least three hundred pounds—and I knew that in order to do anything at all with him, I'd have to field dress him where he lay.

Out came my old worn Buck knife, and I rolled Mr. Bear over on his back. He smelled strong—a dank, rich, wilderness odor. It lay heavy in the thick salt air.

The job of field dressing the beast took between fifteen and twenty minutes, during which time I noticed that the lungs, heart, and liver had all been smashed by my bullets. The chest cavity was full of blood.

Then I rolled him over onto his stomach to drain and began dragging him across the rocks down to the canoe. I wasn't sure if I was going to be able to get him into the canoe, but I also knew that I really didn't have much choice. I was alone and the tide was coming in fast.

In such situations, a man finds that normal physical expectations don't count for much. You do what you have to do. I did. With a couple of heaves, I picked up that bear and dumped him into the canoe. Alaska does this sort of thing to a man.

There wasn't much room left in the canoe for me, but I crawled in and began to paddle back to camp. The tide had risen a couple of feet in the hour or so since I'd left camp. What had been a mudflat earlier now was the most direct route back to camp. I was able to paddle to within fifty yards of where all of the gear lay.

Leaving the bear in the canoe, I walked across the spongy ground to my tent, rummaged through the food cache, and slapped together a quick lunch. The sky began clearing and the world surrounding the bay was transformed by light.

I sat there in camp, going over the details of the stalk, etching them deeper and deeper into my memories, writing them on the pages of my journal, feeling them, nurturing them, pulling the power from them. Mountain goats quietly grazed high among the rocks just across the bay. Geese called. Loons dipped and dived in the clear water. Occasionally there was a rumble as snow or rocks slipped down cliffs.

Everything was in order. The world was as it should be. There had been an encounter between man and bear. The bear had been killed. And as for the hunter . . . there was now a tale to be told. For indeed it is the tale which above all lives on, beyond both the man and the beast. Only the tale dwells in the realm of immortality. Only through the magic of its telling is the spirit of the hunt passed down through humankind's tumbling generations.

Afterglow

Summer nights in the Deep South wrap around you like a blanket. The air is thick and sticky. Stars are dim and fuzzy. There is a stillness of sorts but it's all an illusion because stuff starts to stir in Dixie as the sun begins to tuck itself to bed.

Just as the light starts to dim and the thunderheads turn yellow and the lawn mowers are shut off, mothers start calling wayward kids back to the nest. There's a sort of music to their calls, and even a harmony to it as all the mothers chime in about the same time, always calling with the young'n's first name, and regardless of the name, drawing it out into two syllables, hard on the first one and falling on the second: "Ro . . . bert" or "Do . . . on" or "Mi . . . ke." "Y'all come on in now and wash up for dinner." And if there's no response after a couple of minutes, adding the second name to indicate that she means business and is reaching for the fly swatter: "Robert Andrew!" or "Donald Calvert!" or "Michael Patrick!" "Get on in here right now, dinner's getting cold!" (Pity the poor boy whose mother finally resorted to calling him with all three names!)

Up from the creek banks, out of the barns and sewer culverts, and along dusty roads, kids start streaming home, some with fishing poles in hand, others with BB guns, some with dogs, some without. After stern warnings to wash their feet before coming inside, the air is full of the sound of water from hoses on porch steps and into water bowls (for the dogs), followed by the creaking and slamming of screened doors.

Then come the insects. Mosquitos and lightning bugs are the first, just at dusk as rabbits slip out from the edge of the iris patch down past the garden, and nighthawks flap overhead. Then the locusts crank up and begin their incessant whining from high in the branches of ancient walnuts and oaks, and the crickets start chirping from the wet spot by the faucet that drips. By then the older, teenaged boys have come back home from a day of rambling, or fishing, or working their summer jobs. They plop down at kitchen tables, wolf down cold fried chicken, sliced tomatoes, and large glasses of milk, and then, switching gears, they start scratching around in garages and sheds and loading boats and other gear into the backs of pickup trucks and onto the tops of old junk cars.

They know that beyond the backyards, out across the pastures, and back in the woods, another world is unfolding. Catfish are starting to stir. Bass are beginning to prowl. Snakes are slithering over logs and mudflats. Raccoons and mink are snuffling around the banks of ditches and creeks. Bullfrogs are climbing up out of their hidey holes and hunkering down for a long night of snapping up bugs and other hapless small critters that venture too close. The boys gather in small groups or pairs, crank up their cars and trucks, and head out for a night of adventure and mystery almost beyond imagining to those who have settled down in their air-conditioned living rooms.

It was a wonderful thing to be a teenage boy in the Deep South. The guys I ran around with were all in church or scouts with me and we'd pretty well proven ourselves to our parents. We never betrayed real trust, but we did push the edge. That's just part of growing up. And it was frog hunting that generally took us to the limits of that edge.

There's a sweetness to life when you're seventeen years old, growing an inch a month, muscled out, and have reflexes so fast that they amaze even you. There's a special quality to days (and nights!) when you're rambling around with your buddies, not looking for trouble but prepared (you think) for it if it comes. And this is especially so when you're loaded up in the old car on a steamy July night, with a boat lashed on top and batteries, headlights, and even a gun or two stuffed into the trunk. Four teenage boys in a rebuilt Plymouth hitting the road at 9:00 p.m. is a recipe for adventuring.

There were two places where we generally went frog hunting. One was an old ditch near the town of Keo, Arkansas, and the other was Faulkner Lake, just outside of North Little Rock. The Keo ditch required a

boat. Faulkner Lake did not. If we were out for a whooping good time we went to the Keo ditch. If we were in
a predatory frame of mind, wanting to slip around quietly, stalking our prey and sidestepping cottonmouths
(the danger element added spice to the night), we went
to the backwaters of Faulkner Lake.

My primary frogging buddy was Sam Gates. Sam had
a car (the old Plymouth, fittingly named "The Green
Slime") and the most perfect spirit of adventure I've
ever experienced in a man. He loved the night and he
loved rambling. When we went to the Keo ditch, Sam
would haul his father's little ten-foot aluminum flatbottom boat. I had a three h.p. Johnson outboard motor. We
had another friend, Ted Crowly, who owned a tractor
battery and a headlight on a handle. It could practically
burn the eyes out of a frog at fifty yards . . . Lord, it was
bright! We'd generally call one or two other buddies to
come along, Don Flynn, Aniel House, Mike Kelly, or Joe
Peceny. The boat would hold three people comfortably
but we generally went with four and occasionally with
five people in it. The water in the ditch was only about
waist deep in most spots and never more than chest
deep, so tipping the boat over or falling out wasn't a real
concern to us. During midsummer, the ditch ran low (if
it ran at all), and there were muddy banks on both sides
of the channel.

We scheduled our arrival for about two hours after
sundown (around 11:00 p.m.). This gave us time to get
home from work (Sam and I were lifeguards at local
swimming pools; our frogging buddies worked con-

struction), eat supper, get our stuff together, pick folks up, and drive the hour it took to get to the bridge. From experience, we'd discovered that "frog time" was at least two hours after "people time." Midnight to us was only 10:00 p.m. to frogs. For some reason, frogs just took their merry sweet time getting up out of their loafing spots where they hunkered down in the mud to escape the hot Arkansas sun. But, after the sun had been down a couple of hours and the world had cooled off a little, those muddy ditch banks would have bullfrogs all along them, and this would continue until nearly dawn.

The limit was twelve frogs per person per night. Some of those frogs were real monsters, too. They weren't the "pip-squeak" frogs that you see packaged in grocery stores, the ones that people take the hind legs from and discard the rest. No sir. In addition to huge back legs, these frogs had meat on the back and front legs as big as chicken wings. We skinned and dressed out our frogs just like we dressed out squirrels, and some were as big as squirrels. Occasionally there would be one that would weigh nearly two pounds!

The first order of business when we got to the bridge over the ditch was to get the boat in the water. The ditch bank was steep and slippery, but that was all part of the business. We'd end up covered with mud and scratched by blackberry thorns, but being the "blood and guts" guys that we were, we took it all in stride. Then came the outboard motor, then the battery and light, then paddles, the gun, and the frog box. These last two items deserve special mention.

When we first started frog hunting it became obvious to us that for every frog there was also a snake. We knew the difference between poisonous snakes (usually cottonmouths) and your general, run-of-the-mill water snake. Mostly what we saw were cottonmouths, and they were as nasty and as mean as the devil. When we hunted frogs in the Keo ditch the snakes would swim up to us and try to crawl into the boat. We'd beat them off with boat paddles. Finally, one of the team brought a .25 caliber automatic pistol. It seemed at first to be just the thing: small, rapid-fire, multiple shots. But while it was fast and loud and easy to tote along, all it did was splash water around the snake because we could rarely hit anything with it. And since a snake cannot hear, we might as well have been throwing rocks or marbles at it. We still needed the boat paddles to defend ourselves, in spite of our "cannon." It was sort of like using bayonets and shovels in trench warfare after the bullets are all used up! So we decided to use a .22 rifle. This was a little better. At least we had a better sighting plane with the longer barrel, and could sometimes hit the snake. But hitting the snake did not always stop the snake, and again we'd be back to swinging boat paddles to keep from getting chewed up by "Mr. No-shoulders." The situation was getting critical. So, on a whim one night, I brought along an old single-shot bolt-action .410 shotgun. Our snake problems ended that night. It was a rough-and-tumble little gun, and, loaded with a half ounce of #7½ shot, it sent many a cottonmouth twisting (sometimes cut in half) to the bottom of the ditch. We named the little gun "the comforter." And truly it was.

The frog box was a marvelous contraption, simple in design, but absolutely the difference between a "Ford" and a "Cadillac" frog hunt. Many of our friends used old burlap sacks to put their frogs in. While this works, you're always having to tie or hold the bag shut and then when you want to sort or cull your frogs, you end up having frogs jump out of the bag and then you have a real mess.

Our box was a simple frame affair with hardware cloth tacked around the sides. On the top was a hinged door big enough to let you pop your frog inside, and yet small enough so that it took a pretty wise and observant frog to see the hole in the dark of a summer's night. If they hopped around in the box while you were sorting or culling, they just rammed their noses against the sides of the box, because your hand and arm were in the hole, blocking their escape.

This brings up another important point. Most people catch frogs with a multiprong gig, which is a sort of spear. A speared frog is not one that you can cull and release. But that wasn't a factor in our frog hunting. When we frog hunted from the boat out on the Keo ditch, we caught the frogs with our hands (thus the concern about snakes and the experimentation with the various guns). If at the end of a night's hunt there were unwanted frogs, we simply dumped them back into the ditch unharmed.

Once everything was in the boat, we loaded ourselves and pushed off into the murky water. It would
be very, very dark because you can't hunt frogs when
there's much of a moon. Lightning bugs would be sparkling all around us. There would be a stillness broken
only by the "karoomp" of a bullfrog bellowing somewhere along the ditch. But the stillness was soon broken as I cranked the little outboard motor to life. It typically coughed a few times and finally caught and started
humming, blue smoke from the two-cycled engine drifting out across the water.

Most of the time I operated the outboard motor. In
the middle seat was the man with the light. He also
operated the frog box unless there were four of us on
the hunt. In the front of the boat was the grabber. The
whole crew operated like a finely tuned, well-oiled
machine. The man with the light would spot a frog and
keep the light on it. I'd drive right up to the frog. The
other guy in the middle, the one handling the frog box,
would have the little shotgun ready, just in case of a
snake emergency. The grabber would be on his knees
on the front seat of the boat, bending forward, balanced
and with hands ready. Just as we were about to make
impact on the muddy bank, I'd spin the little outboard
around (it had a 360° turn), stall the boat and be backing
out into the ditch. The grabber would grab the frog and
we'd be long gone from the spot by the time the snake
beside the frog, and there usually was one, knew what
had happened. The grabber would turn around, frog in
hand, and deposit the critter into the opening of the frog

box, which immediately was slammed shut by the man riding shotgun. Before the frog even had time to say "howdy" to the other frogs in the box, we'd be on our way to the next frog.

On a good night we could get thirty to forty frogs, but most nights we ended up with a couple of dozen. There were things that slowed us down and limited our catch. There were mud bars to pull over and brush jams to get through. Sometimes, when we were working around an overhanging branch to get to a frog, someone would be so intent on the frog that they wouldn't notice the branch. So we'd have to go pick up the guy who got knocked out of the boat. Sometimes a snake would fall into the boat and we'd all have to abandon ship. If I'd left the motor running, we'd then have to splash and swim in the muddy soup of the ditch, trying to catch the boat again. Then we'd have to attend to the snake and this could take some time. One night, the snake situation got so bad that in a moment of focused aggression, one of our crew actually shot a hole in the bottom of the boat. Seeing water spouting up into the boat, and at 3:00 a.m. not thinking very clearly, he shot another hole so that the water would run back out. He swears to this day that he didn't do it. But there were three witnesses.

This same sportsman, on a dare, grabbed a great blue heron one night as it stood transfixed in our light. We're all lucky to be alive as a result. The heron was grabbed halfway up the neck, leaving plenty of neck for pecking, wings free to flap, and long legs with sharp claws to kick and then some.

That bird tore into us with a viciousness I've never experienced since. Even when our buddy turned it loose it still attacked with fury. Its five-inch-long beak was a dagger and that bird knew how to use it. Finally, wearying of its assault and the carnage it had wrought, it flapped away into the darkness, but not before leaving one last insult upon the defeated. It unleashed the full contents of its bowels all over us. There must have been over a gallon of that white, slimy, stinky stuff splattered on us and the boat. To this day, all hands who were aboard that ship have a certain sort of respect for herons not common to the general public.

On another night I witnessed an Irishman walk on water. We were a well-oiled team that night. I was chief engineer, driving the boat. Sam was torpedo man in the bow, both "tubes" armed and ready to grab the frogs (and doing an exceptional job of it as I recall). Ted Crowly was our radar man, in charge of searching the battle lane for prey. Michael Patrick Kelly was in charge of the brig and all prisoners taken, and did double duty as the officer in charge of the artillery.

As southern boys, we all had grown up with snakes and had a deep and abiding respect for them. But with Michael Patrick Kelly that "respect" assumed dimensions of special proportions. Although he loved the South, he dreamed of northern lands where there were no snakes. He was haunted by snakes in his dreams. A stick beside a path would be sufficient cause for a jump. He typically shot half as many squirrels as the rest of us on early October hunts because squirrels live in trees and his eyes were mostly on the ground. We all gave Mike a hard time about his fear of snakes, but in reality, he was just a lot closer to the truth of possibilities than the rest of us were willing to admit.

On that very special night, the night of the miracle, with Mike and Ted in the middle seat of the boat, me driving and Sam grabbing, we approached a big limb hanging over the water. I could see Mike beginning to shift on his seat. He knew that snakes will often stretch out on a branch like that and when disturbed (as when a boat passes under them in the dark of the night with a light shining), they instinctively fall into the water, or boat, depending on whether or not the boat is still under them. It had very rarely occurred with us, but it *had* happened.

It was then that I saw the face of evil. Ted Crowly turned and looked at me and smiled . . . a strange sort of smile . . . and then quietly, smoothly, slipped off his belt. I held my breath, knowing what was about to happen. Mike was more and more nervous as we neared the branch. Ted began to shake (from laughter). Dutifully, I continued on course (also shaking). Then, at the proper moment, Ted's belt flopped, every so gently, leather cool to the touch, across Mike's lightly clad back, neck, and right shoulder. There was a subhuman utterance that sprang forth from deep within Mike's oversoul, and which caused the hair on the backs of our necks to stand up. The boat hardly wobbled as Mike abandoned ship, screeching, making for the shore and, although the water was probably up to Mike's neck, only the lower half of his boots got wet.

Once the reality of the situation was clear to Mike, terrible things were said. In fact, things so terrible that we were fearful for our lives and elected to leave Mike in the dark, with whatever slithered along the mud banks for company, until he calmed down. Rational thought soon stimulated a cooling of the temper with which Mike is culturally blessed. He was back in the boat in less than three minutes, but with the clear understanding that for the rest of the night, Ted's belt would stay in the frog box.

Nights on Faulkner Lake were different. They were magic. Spirits (and other things) prowled through the mist and fog and stillness. In June, before the vegetation was so thick you couldn't see frogs (or snakes), it was already too hot to wear hip boots, so we just wore old blue jeans and worn-out tennis shoes. Mike typically chose not to accompany us to Faulkner Lake, citing other responsibilities, etc. And he was wise. When, on occasion, I passed the lake during daylight hours, snakes virtually dripped from the brush-choked area where we hunted frogs. At night, the only ones we saw were those caught in the beam of our light. We tried to forget about all the unseen ones. It was a game we played with ourselves.

Sometimes I hunted alone, but mostly I hunted with Sam or with another fellow named Mike Garner. And when the three of us were together, there was a synergism of spirit and adventure to rival all others. We weren't foolish, but we did push and push hard. Sometimes we'd be up to our armpits out in the lake stalking a frog and have to freeze as a cottonmouth swam by, perhaps only inches away. For some reason, however, the snakes didn't bother us when we were out there like that. They were also focused on frogs, and as long as we didn't mess with them, they didn't mess with us. That's small comfort to a frog hunter, but it seemed to be the case. The same snake during the day-time would have attacked just for the pure joy of being the meanest snake in the swamp. But at night, it was a different situation, a different realm of being . . . a different rhythm to life. When we were out wading around in that lake, never once did we have a snake show any *real* aggression. Mostly they just seemed curious.

When hunting Faulkner Lake, we did not use a boat, we did not use a strong spotlight, and we did not catch frogs with our hands. We waded, used small nine-volt battery-powered headlights, and carried gigs on long bamboo poles. Our gigs, however, were not pronged spears. They were spring-activated clamps that we had filed down so that they would have hair triggers and close completely rather than just sort of clamp shut.

Faulkner Lake hunts were quiet hunts. There was no noise from an outboard motor. There was no loud talking, hooping and hollering. We moved with stealth through the night, searching the shoreline and stumps for the telltale red-orange glow of a frog's eye. We stalked eyes, not frogs.

When an eye was spotted, especially if there was any sort of light in the sky like a sliver of a moon or bright stars, we planned the stalk so that we would not be silhouetted against the sky. It was important also to keep the light on the eye. If the light drifted away, the frog would spot you and be gone. But if you moved ever so slowly, ever so quietly, working with and from the shadows, you could get up to the frog and, with a quick thrust, slam the trigger of the clamp gig into the frog's back, causing it to snap shut and hold your frog.

As rough as this may sound, frogs were rarely injured. Mostly they were just shoved down into the mud as the clamp closed around them. A little swishing in the water and they were as slick and clean and lively as ever. Sometimes when we thrust at them they'd jump before we could pin them down. The tale that would win a night would be of snatching a frog right out of the air as it jumped to make its escape. Sometimes the clamp would only close on a leg and you'd have to be quick or else the frog would reach back with the other legs and pull free.

After most catches, with a frog secure in the clamp, I'd just hold out the frog on the end of the gig pole for a moment or so, perhaps swish it around in the water a little to clean it up, but mostly just letting the rush within me settle, letting the whole of the experience sort of soak in. It was marvelous. It was wild. It was primitive. It was really me and I loved it.

Sometimes, especially early in the season when the water had warmed but after a late season cool front had moved into the region, the frogs would be "float-ers." They wouldn't come to shore but rather would hang out in the water, where it was warm. These frogs were especially hard to stalk because they could feel the ripples of your approach. Just as you were making your final, careful approach, they'd sink and there was nothing you could do about it. They also were tough to catch because there was nothing underneath them except water, and so trying to trip the spring of the gig required a sort of snap of the wrist rather than a good, clean, forceful, direct snatch as would be possible on a shoreline frog sitting on the mud.

But regardless of conditions, the entire affair of frog hunting on that lake was wonderful beyond words. There was a special smell that drifted up from the lake, a smell that was a mixture of fish and mud and decay that thrilled me. At 2:00 a.m., there was also a special sort of rhythm to life, a careful, deliberate pace that wasn't part of the daytime world. I saw all sorts of stuff. I wasn't alone out there. I shared the world with other night creatures. There were raccoons, mink, and musk-rats out and about. Even in that era of few deer, I saw lots of them, and they were always special to me. Of course there were also the snakes, but they just came with the turf.

One night on Faulkner Lake was particularly mem-orable. There had been a lot of rain the previous day or two. As a result, the lake had backed up across a soy-bean field. The field had not yet been planted because the farmer was waiting for the spring rains and flooding to subside. Out in the field there were still old soybeans left over from the previous year.

I was hunting with Sam Gates and Mike Garner along the edge of the lake. After swimming across a ditch that emptied into the lake, we ended up in this soybean field. We looked across the field where water met land and saw no frogs. But something caught Mike's eye. There had been a swirl in the water. Mike quietly moved over to where he'd seen the swirl and suddenly made a lunge with his gig. When he brought it up, he had a yellow bullhead catfish that weighed about a pound. That's pretty big for a bullhead catfish. It fact, the world record is something on the order of four pounds. He hollered for us to come over and take a look. When we got there we looked out into the shallow water, and it was teeming with catfish that had come up out of the lake and were in the field eating old soybeans.

Being the opportunistic "sportsmen" that we were, we quickly switched gears and started gigging catfish. Because our gigs were not spears but rather clamp gigs, technically we figured that we were legal. All we were doing was "gaffing" the fish, not "gigging" them. In a couple of hours, we had three burlap sacks full of catfish and were on our way home.

It was always great to come home as the first lights of dawn filled the summer sky. As a lifeguard, I didn't have to get to work until around 1:00 p.m., so a dawn docking still gave me enough time to get a good "night's" sleep and lunch before work. My mother and father would be up stirring around the house as we pulled into the driveway, and my father would come out to see how we'd done. Although he almost never went out with me on these forays, he knew what they were all about because he'd done this sort of stuff back when he was growing up in the delta region of northeast Arkansas. He knew that these frog hunting trips were part and parcel of a young man's maturation process in the Deep South. He encouraged the trips and always congratulated us on what we'd caught.

We'd haul our sacks out to the backyard, hook up the water hose, and go get knives and pans. The frogs (and occasional catfish) were skinned and cleaned out on the grass, usually with a bird dog and little brother watching. We'd pull the nerves from the frog legs (so that they would not jump out of the pans when they were put in hot grease), and fillet or steak the catfish. Then we'd package and freeze the catch (unless there was a meal planned very soon).

By the time we were finished, my mom would have a breakfast waiting. She knew how to win boys' hearts. Sometimes the guys I hunted frogs with would end up sleeping at my house rather than going home, in order to save time and to get just a little more sleep before they went to work later in the day. My two teenage sisters liked having the guys in the house, and sometimes I wondered if my hunting buddies were slogging around with me for frogs or for the chance to be around my sisters. It was all sort of jumbled up, but quite frankly it really didn't matter one way or the other . . . until one morning.

We'd gotten in a little early, around 3:30, and decided that we'd wait until daylight to clean the frogs. We had some real dandies and, in deference to their trophy status, decided that our frogs would be safer inside the house than outside of it. There was only one logical place to store them—in the bathtub.

We put about six inches of water in the tub so that the frogs would swim (we hoped) rather than jump, and then, for good measure, we pulled the shower curtain. If a frog jumped, it would hit the curtain and fall back into the tub, or so we thought.

Sometime around 6:30 that morning there was a scream that obviously came from one of my sisters in the bathroom. My buddies and I jumped out of our sacks, and rushed down the hall to see what was going on.

My oldest sister, Lynn, a year younger than me, was standing on the top of the commode seat in the bathroom. Tucked behind the utility, back in a secluded corner, was one of our trophy frogs. My sister, sleepy-eyed and drowsy, had taken a seat. After a few moments, she'd heard some splashing in the tub behind the shower curtain. Then there had been a sort of guttural grumbling and a cold, wet thing bumped into her ankles and let out a bellow.

Once the situation had calmed, it was obvious that the admiration from my sisters, once enjoyed by my hunting buddies, was now lost to them on this home front. Frogs, from this moment on, would have to stay outside, regardless of trophy status. All frog hunters, most especially us, would forevermore live under the cloud of suspicion. The tall, lanky "princes" who once accompanied me home from our nighttime forays into the unknown now were to be relegated to the stature of adopted brothers, and to be treated as such. No more starry eyes for these characters, but rather the direct (albeit sometimes affectionate) word from a sister who had decided that *her* princes really live in another world—a world that did not center around mucky places and cold, slimy things.

This clarified frog hunting tremendously for me, because, to the man, the entire crew hung in there with the hunting and with me. It was obvious where *their* priorities were. For what can compare with the allure of a night out, corking around with the guys you like the best, especially when it's spent in some of the gosh-awfullest, most wonderfully wild, sucking, oozing, snake-ridden backwaters known to humankind. This is the sort of stuff that creates brothers, regardless of whether or not there's kinship or a sister involved.

But my sisters? Well, they *are* daughters of the South, and with time they have mellowed in this realm. Now, strangely (or perhaps not so strangely), frog hunting is *very* important to them, for *their* teenage sons have been out there doing it. My sisters recognize that, through this business of frog hunting, their sons have experienced a very important rite of passage. They have engaged the wild around them and the wild within themselves. They have ventured forth into the unknown without counsel. They have endured and survived and been tested. Choices have been made in the darkest hours. In the face of danger they have held firm. Woven among all this are the threads of humor and mischief that form the essence, the sparkle, of the human spirit. And the sons have returned, time and again, sailors home from the sea, hunters home from the hills, victorious—a bit tussled perhaps, but victorious nevertheless.

I have discussed this business in depth with my sisters. Finally, they just sighed, shook their heads, and with some reservation, eventually concurred with me that, even from a feminine perspective, a man's first venture into manhood, at least the most significant one, may very well be in a ditch.

Infected by
Old River Chute

Just after I finished the fourth grade, back in 1961, when I was ten years old, my father accepted a call to be the minister at Park Hill Christian Church (Disciples of Christ) in North Little Rock, Arkansas. We'd been up in Kentucky for several years while he finished seminary, but Arkansas was "home." My mother's family was in the Ozarks and my father's was in the Delta. It didn't really matter to me where we lived just as long as there was a place for me to ramble in the wild.

North Little Rock in the 1960s fit that ticket. It was right at the edge of the hills, and the community where the parsonage was located had plenty of woods around it for me to roam in, lakes scattered everywhere for me to fish in, and places (legal and otherwise) for me to go swimming. I connected with the place very quickly and soon linked up with a gang of other boys to ramble around with.

Summers in Arkansas back then were so wonderful that they probably should have been made illegal. There was an abundance of sunshine, lots of lizards to shoot at with your BB gun, and crawfish in the creeks just waiting to be caught. You could go around in your bare feet and without a shirt on just about anywhere. Fishing down at the lake, about five minutes away from my house, was great in the mornings. Local swimming beaches opened at noon and didn't close until 8:00 p.m. And then, after supper and a little begging and dealing with my parents, frog gigging kicked in and went on sometimes until midnight (or later). There were Boy Scout camps, free movies for kids at a local theater two afternoons a week, church youth groups with all sorts of picnics and other activities, and scads of woods, creeks, rocky bluffs, and lakes to explore. It was really a sort of paradise for a boy.

But, after two years of this paradise, when I was twelve years old, by the middle of July, with more than a month to go before school started, I was as restless as a fox in a forest fire. I was saturated, overwhelmed, exhausted, burned brown by the sun, soles of my feet thick and leathery from walking barefoot, hair bleached nearly white, and ankles scarred by mosquito bites and poison ivy. Well tempered and honed by scuffles with my buddies, I'd started to pester my sisters, gave my younger brother little if any breathing room; I'd built a tree house and covered it with "wallpaper" of questionable materials (e.g., foldouts from "men's" magazines I'd found in a trash dump). From time to time I'd stirred up trouble down at the swimming beach, "borrowed" neighbors' boats to go fishing and swimming from, and usually came home late for supper after a day of rebel rousing with my buddies. I'd get so swept up in the whirlwind of activities that filled my days that when my folks put me to bed at night I'd toss and turn and stay awake sometimes until around midnight. There was no opportunity for stuff to "settle." By sunrise, with dew still on the ground, I'd be long gone again, in search of new adventures. What I needed was space and time to myself . . . and quiet.

So my folks shipped me off for a few weeks near the end of summer to go stay with my grandmother, who lived out in the middle of the Delta in a farming community called Whitton, in Mississippi County, about an hour northwest of Memphis. It was a check, of sorts, on the crescendo that had built up in me. A different pace was required to still the waters, a different prescription to bring some balance and order into the heart and soul of a renegade.

I didn't complain. I didn't balk. I was always ready for the change and a chance to be with my grandmother. I loved my grandmother (I was the oldest grandson) and I loved to be out there on her farm, poking around the countryside, hitching rides with my uncle Bob in his pickup truck as he made his rounds, riding his big Tennessee walking horse on dusty roads as evening crept across the land, sitting on the porch with my grandmother watching the sun set over Dead Timber Lake, listening to the chickens out in the yard, and then, as darkness fell and the nighthawks began to swoop and mosquitoes began to swarm, going inside to sit at her table and stuff myself on fried chicken, sliced tomatoes, summer squash, fresh rolls, slaw, and apple pie.

There wasn't really any need for extra entertainment. I'd go take a bath and then come out to sit with my grandmother in her living room, watching the *Red Skelton Show* or something else on her TV and listening to the crunch of gravel as a car passed on the road out past the front yard. It was quiet and calm and lonesome out there. I loved it. I still do.

During the days, I'd just set out to see what was going on, around the farm, in the old tractor sheds, down in front of the store, up at my uncle's barn, over at the cotton gin. I was then and still am a first-class "piddler." I spent hours just kicking in the bushes, or poking around the garden, or walking down a dirt road. If there was a bridge over a ditch, I often spent an entire day sitting on the edge of the bridge with my legs dangling over the edge, watching turtles and snakes and dragonflies. Sometimes when I'd be out roaming around, I'd carry the old single-shot .22 rifle a family friend in Kentucky had given me, and shoot at turtles or pretend I was a marine on patrol, shooting at dirt clots in the turn rows of the cotton fields, pretending that they were the enemy. I couldn't afford the expensive "long rifle" cartridges back then so only shot standard velocity "shorts." They cost forty cents for a box of fifty bullets. I didn't really have any money when I was staying at my grandmother's house, but there always seemed to be a box of .22 shorts that would show up when my ammo supply started to run low.

My uncle Bob, who had been a soldier in China during World War II, had an uncanny ability to know just what a boy needed. And it was this wisdom from my uncle Bob that introduced me to something that changed my life forever.

The whole landscape of the Delta where our family farm was located had been sculptured by the Mississippi River, over thousands and perhaps millions of years. Although we were in Arkansas, the soil we farmed came from Iowa, Minnesota, Missouri, and Indiana. It had been deposited over the landscape by countless floods from the Mississippi River and its tributaries. It was deep and black and rich and if you spit on it you would clone yourself. It was that fertile.

The Mississippi River has always been a restless one, whipping back and forth across the land, carving and abandoning channels, leaving here and there remnants of itself in the form of oxbow lakes, sloughs, and swamps. The closer you get to the river, the more you begin to realize all of this. And by the time you actually get to the river, you realize that it isn't always just one channel, but in fact there can be several channels, some larger and more powerful than others, but all of them still alive and kicking. It's a heck of a big old river and many a head has ducked under its surface, never to rise again. It will suck your boat under in a sudden whirlpool. It will whip you and toss you and do anything it can to remind you that you are just a tiny speck of insignificant life, and that it doesn't care about you at all. For a twelve-year-old boy in Arkansas, it was just about the most awesome thing imaginable.

So when my uncle Bob drove up to my grandmother's front porch one hot, sticky evening after supper and announced that we were going "over to the river" to fish the next morning, my heart began to pound. The river? THE river? My mind swirled with images of busted boats, drowned boys, huge catfish and alligator gars, and turtles that could snap off a man's leg. I didn't even know that you *could* fish on the river. And I couldn't wait. Buddy, I sensed adventure of the first order, and when it came to adventuring, you could count me in. Let me at that river!

The next morning my grandmother woke me up at 5:00 and had breakfast already on the way. My uncle showed up with my two cousins, Andy and Greg, about fifteen minutes later, and we all had breakfast. My grandmother had packed lunches for all of us, and I noticed that there were a couple of extras. She said they were for Joel D. and his boy Mikey.

Joel D. Linley was my uncle's hired hand and sharecropper. He was a big man, powerfully built, with strong hands and strong laughter. He'd taught me how to pull tushes from newly born pigs and how to weld down at my uncle's shop and how to drive a tractor. He was a poacher, a trapper, an owner of illegal fish nets and traps, and he had a boat and motor that we were going to use for fishing that day. He lived in an old house under some huge walnut trees back off a dirt road, not far from the fields that owned him and ruled his life from March through October. He was dirt poor, full of spirit, rough as a cob, and he loved boys. There were no Boy Scouts in that part of Arkansas back then, but had there been, he would have been a perfect scoutmaster. He was a man like no other I had ever known at the time, and like few I've ever met since. I idolized him and pledged secretly to myself that someday I was going to grow up to be just like him. He was a crusty old scoundrel, but the crust of Joel D. was like that over an apple pie. Break through it and there's treasure to behold.

My uncle Bob and Joel D. were two peas in a pod. I never saw two men get along so well. They worked day after day together on the farm, long days, hot days, cold days, dusty days, muddy days, relentlessly trying to drag a living into the world of their families from the earth that they tended. They were master mechanics, accomplished chemists, weathermen without peer, and economists of the highest order. They knew the land and crops and banks, and agricultural suppliers, and markets and politics. Joel D. did not desire riches. He just wanted to be free and outside. The life of a share-cropper suited him just fine. The millions they made over the years went to my uncle, as was befitting and proper for a southern planter. There was never any question. Never any tension. It's just the way things were. But Joel D. and his family never lacked for anything, including education for the children, medical attention, decent cars; anything that smoothed over the bumps, he got. That too was just the way things were in the old Whitton community.

When we got to Joel D.'s house he and Mikey had the boat already dragged out from behind the house, and there was a big white outboard motor lying on the ground beside it. There was an aluminum Coleman ice chest, two minnow buckets, three hand-carved cypress boat paddles, about a dozen well-cured cane poles, and a beat-up "Buddy" tackle box.

The boat was thrown into the bed of the pickup truck. Then came an old tire which was the cushion for the outboard motor. After the motor and gas can were put in, all the other gear was loaded. Uncle Bob and Joel D. would ride in the cab of the truck. The four boys would ride in the back and, according to Joel D., "serve as ballast."

We pulled out of Joel D.'s driveway just as the sun rose above the woods behind his house. Doves were flitting around and landing along the dusty road. Tractors and drivers were already hard at work in the fields. The air was cool and fresh on us in the back of the truck, but we were under no illusion as to what the heat would be like later on. This was midsummer in the Delta. It would likely be a hundred degrees in the shade about 3:00 p.m. But for now, the new day was gorgeous, wind whipping at us, and us shouting at each other just to see if we could hear each other.

After about forty-five minutes, Uncle Bob turned off the main gravel road onto a road that snaked its way down through some woods. The woods were like a jungle, thick, green, full of no telling what sort of crawling, poisonous things: "copper-mouthed rattle heads" no doubt, and wild hogs that would just as soon eat a boy for breakfast as anything. Then we pulled up to a stop and got out. There was an old shanty house tucked back off the side of the road with a porch and a big red "pop" cooler sitting on it. There was a thermometer advertising Wonder Bread and wooden crates that obviously served as chairs. The inside of the place was very dark and musty smelling. In the back was a cooler with glass doors, and on its shelves were all sorts of meats that could be sliced for sandwiches. Out back was a big cattle watering trough that served as a minnow barrel. We bought six dozen minnows, an extra package of hooks, some cork bobbers, and a sack of ice. We also paid fifty cents to launch our boat.

I walked down to where we were to launch the boat and for the first time realized that where we were going to fish was something other than I'd imagined. Rather than some huge, rolling, monster of a river, this was gentle, quiet, with just a little current, lots of old treetops along the banks, and, at this early hour, lots of shade. It was called Old River Chute, and was part of the Mississippi River, but was a side channel. It looped out of sight about a quarter of a mile either direction but with the current, obviously it was connected to someplace, something, else. I was both amazed and delighted. This place *looked* fishy and *smelled* fishy and it didn't look like the sort of place that sucked down boys and drowned them. I was a strong swimmer, having recently done the mile swim at Boy Scout camp. I'd been prepared to earn the Boy Scouts' gold Honor Medal for saving the lives of everyone after the river had swallowed up our boat, but the water before me certainly didn't hold the same danger as I'd imagined the night before. I was a little disappointed that I wasn't going to be able to become a hero that day but, as boys will, quickly shifted gears and focused on the world, and the river, that lay in front of me. I didn't know what kind of fish might be in there but it really didn't matter.

The boat was only fourteen feet long but it was more than big enough for all of us. There were two adults and four medium-sized boys. Joel D. sat in the back seat and operated the motor. Uncle Bob sat in one of the middle seats with my cousin Andy. Cousin Greg and I had another seat and Mikey sat alone in the front seat. We all got situated and settled in, Joel D. cranked up the motor, and finally Mikey untied us and off we went.

It was my first time ever out on a real river. I'd been on lots of creeks, especially back in Kentucky, and the place we swam in at the Boy Scout camp was called a river but really was just a big creek. This, however, was a river, and once on it I realized that what I'd thought earlier about it having a gentle current was totally off base. There was power here on this thing and the boat had to fight its way upstream. When I looked at the water, it seemed that we were going at a pretty good clip, but when I looked at the shore, I was shocked to see how slow we were going.

Soon, however, Joel D. was able to duck back alongside the far bank, and as if by magic the current was almost gone. I'd never thought about a river having different sorts of currents in different places. I'd just thought it all sort of went together. But Joel D. was an old "river rat" and this was his domain. He knew how to tack side to side going up a river so that you minimized the amount of time you had to fight the main force of the current.

I asked him why he went upstream instead of downstream and he laughed and asked me, "What if the motor conks out on us downstream? Are you ready to paddle back upstream? This way, we can always drift back home."

In the first fifteen minutes that I was on the river with Joel D. that July morning, he taught me, a twelve-year-old boy, two fundamental aspects of travel on a river that I still use to this day and which, as a professor at Mississippi State University, I pass along to my graduate students in our river fisheries research: always try to plan your trip so that you start out traveling upstream; then, don't fight the current, cut it. Practical wisdom from a seasoned, practical man. Little did Joel D. know that his wisdom would someday became fundamental to the logistics of many successful Ph.D. research projects.

I settled into the ride on the river, knowing that I was safe in the hands of our pilot. I watched the water tug at snags and bite at bends. I saw where it shoaled over underwater sandbars and gravel bars, and where it swirled and eddied upon first breaking back into clear channel. I wondered about why sandbars were on the inside of bends and steep banks were on the outside. Joel D. said it was because the current piled up there and cut the banks. That was why so many snags were in the bends. As the river chewed away at the bank, trees just fell in. The bars were formed because the current wasn't strong enough on the inside of the bend to keep things moving along.

"Where do we fish?" I asked. I knew about ponds and lakes and creeks, but rivers were a mystery to me.

"Depends on what you want," Joel D. answered. "If you want catfish, this time of day, go to those cut banks where the current is swift and the water is deep and there's plenty of cover. But at night, go to the shoals and shallows for catfish. Today, we're not fishing for catfish. We're going for crappie. They will be in quiet water where there are some old treetops sticking up, and they'll be on the shady side of the river. Maybe when we're done with crappie we'll try for something else."

I then started looking at the land beyond the water. There were shore birds on the mudflats. They'd bob their tails up and down, stick out their heads and run like little quail along the place where mud and water met. There were wild ducks too. I mentioned to my uncle Bob that I thought ducks flew north in the summer and asked him why they were still here. He said that they were "summer ducks" and that their real name was wood ducks. They lived with us down in the South all year. I was amazed at how fast they flew. They made strange squealing noises as they passed over us.

Swallows had holes in the steep banks and Joel D. said they had nests in the holes. There was one bird that Joel D. called a "snake bird" that we saw sitting on a snag with its wings all spread out. Then it fell into the water and disappeared. A little bit later, it popped its head up and started swimming but only showing that head. I didn't know the names of the birds back then, nor did I know the names of the fish or turtles or snakes we saw that day. But I was in love with it all.

I loved the way the river smelled, a mixture of mud and woods and dead fish, and God only knows what other sort of scum and dead stuff. But it all mixed together to make a smell that was rich and wonderful. I loved the way the light played on the water and the forest along the river channels. I loved the flash of sand bars. I loved the slick look of mud bars. I loved the animal tracks when we got out and explored. I didn't know what sort of animals had made the tracks, but Joel D. showed me tracks that he said were mink, otter, and raccoon.

"How do you know?" I asked.

And he just laughed his deep, full-bodied laugh and said it's just a matter of time in the woods.

I wanted that time . . . more and more of it . . . and time on this river . . . all rivers. The names of things didn't matter much to me but there was something else that did. I couldn't describe it but it was sort of a feeling that I had, that being there was right.

After a while we pulled up alongside a bank where the water didn't move much and where it was shady and there were lots of treetops sticking up, a place like Joel D. had said was where crappie lived. I didn't know what a crappie was but it didn't matter. I just wanted to catch one.

We tied fishing line halfway up the cane poles, then wound the line around the poles all the way to the tip where we tied them again very tightly. I asked why we didn't just tie the lines to the tips of the poles, and Joel D. said that it was an insurance policy.

"A what?" I asked.

"Insurance," answered Uncle Bob. "What if you hang into a big ole catfish or something and it busts your pole half in two? It's a lost fish automatic if you only have your line tied to one place on the pole. But with it tied in the middle too, if a big fish breaks your pole, throw the pole over the side and let the fish drag it around awhile. After a bit, it will wear out tugging on that pole and you can go get your fish."

"Insurance," I thought, "a handy thing to have," and I tied my line three times to my pole.

Once everyone was rigged up and ready, the minnow buckets were passed around. There was a little dipper net for each bucket. Uncle Bob said use the net, not your hands, to catch a minnow from the bucket because your hands are not as clean as the net, you probably will smash minnows inside the bucket, and it's harder to catch minnows with your hands.

So, the first chance I got, when I thought nobody was looking, I tried to grab a minnow with my hands. After a while I gave up and used the net. Sometimes technology has its advantages, especially when you want to get your hook into the water and start fishing.

Joel D. instructed all of us not to jerk too hard when the crappie pulled the bobbers under the water. He said that they have really weak mouths and it is easy to rip the hook right out of them. Just go slow and sort of swing the crappie up and out of the water and into the boat.

I watched my bobber and then saw that it was sort of cruising along the surface of the water, but not going under. I thought maybe the current was causing it to drift so just sort of pulled back on it smoothly. But there was a tug on the other end and when I tugged back, it pulled back even harder. I hauled up on the pole and all of a sudden a crappie that weighed about a pound came swinging up and right into the boat.

Once I got my hands on it, I recognized the fish.

"Hey!" I shouted. "I just caught a newlite."

"A what?" asked Uncle Bob.

"A newlite," I said. "We used to catch lots of these up in Kentucky but I haven't caught one in Arkansas yet. This is my first here."

"Son, that's a *crappie*," Uncle Bob said. "They may be newlites in Kentucky but here they are crappie, and congratulations, that one is a dandy."

"O.K., crappie it is," I said. And I baited up again and swung another minnow into a brush top.

For a couple of hours the action was pretty steady and the crappie started to pile up in the ice chest. There were also a couple of bass but they weren't very big, perhaps three-quarters of a pound, nothing more. Then, it was all over . . . just like that. Nothing. No bites. No nibbles. Nothing.

The sun was getting higher. The shade was gone. It was about 10:30 and it was getting hot. The minnows started to die. We needed to stretch our legs. So Joel D. drove the boat over to a sandbar and we all crawled out to do some exploring.

A wild sandbar where nobody has been in a long time can be a wonderful place. There are all sorts of things on a sandbar. There are shells and driftwood begging to be picked up. There are old boards and boat paddles and sometimes chunks of old boats, all bleached in the sun. There are dead fish to poke at with sticks. Back from the water there sometimes are little pools where things get trapped—tadpoles and sometimes fish. Birds hang around these shallows and back up in the shady areas where new forest is forming. There are also deer tracks on occasion. Joel D. called to me and showed me where the deer had come out, probably during the night, to get a drink and wander around.

On one side of the sandbar where we were, there was a bit of current that cut a pretty steep bank. Uncle Bob said for me to be careful because the bank could slip and I'd have to swim and they'd have to go get me with the boat. I got my fishing pole, put on a dead minnow, and swung it out into the current. Almost immediately I caught a fish. It was sort of like half bass, half crappie but had lines running down its side and was sort of golden looking. It was my first yellow bass ever.

Although fairly small, it was a prize for me and I put it in the cooler to take back to show my grandmother.

After about an hour on the sandbar for lunch and stretching, we decided to start on back toward the landing. But we still had some dead minnows. So, once in the boat, we threaded the dead, pale, stiff little fish on our hooks in wads, shortened the distance between bobber and hook, and started drifting out in the middle of the river channel. We didn't need the motor because the current kept us going. Joel D. and Uncle Bob kept us straight with the boat paddles.

All of a sudden, my cousin Andy let out a whoop and there was a tremendous splash as a gar hit his bait. The little cane pole bent and bucked but held. The gar jumped a couple of times and then dived under the boat. Andy hung on with all his might, and finally, the fish came back over to the other side and Joel D. netted it. It was over three feet long, and Joel D. said that it probably weighed more than twelve pounds.

Then we all started hooking gar. But unlike the first one, these mostly didn't stay hooked. We learned that actually getting a hook to set in a gar's bony old mouth is really hard. Unless you just happen to get the hook in the corner of the mouth the gar is probably going to jump a time or two and then turn loose. Eventually, however, we all caught one and threw them in the bottom of the boat where they sloshed around in some of the water we'd splashed in during the day.

By the time we'd drifted near the launch we were hot, tired, and thirsty boys. As boys will, we scrambled out of the boat just as soon as the boat touched the shore and were on our way up to the "pop" chest at the store to get cold drinks. But we were called back to help haul stuff up to the truck before we got very far. There was work to do, especially carrying the cooler full of fish. We'd probably caught twenty-five to thirty crappie and an assortment of other things like drum, bass, and the yellow bass I'd caught on the sandbar.

Only after everything was loaded were we rewarded with a cool drink. My favorite was NuGrape bellywash. It is a sticky sweet purple drink that is supposed to taste like grapes and that has a lot of carbonation. My uncle Bob also got a NuGrape, but everyone else got a Pepsi as I recall.

The ride back to Whitton and grandmother's house was hot and windy. We smelled like old fish slime mixed with gas, our clothes were covered in mud, and our shoes were full of sand. We were sunburned, tired, and very, very happy boys. Grandmother made us go wash ourselves with a garden hose out by the storm cellar before we did anything else. She was wise in the ways of boys. Nothing like being told to get into a water fight with a garden hose to perk us up. We even grabbed our gar and chased each other around with them. Then she brought out a board and some spoons, a butcher knife, and a big cake pan. Andy and Greg would scale the fish. I'd cut off heads and fins. Mikey would wash them and put them in the pan.

When we were done, we left our dirty clothes by the storm cellar, cleaned up with soap, and wrapped ourselves in towels that Grandmother had brought out to us and then went inside to change. While we were changing, we could hear Grandmother in the kitchen, and by the time we were presentable, we could smell cooking fish. Joel D. and Uncle Bob had cleaned up in the bathroom and were already at the table when we got there. There was a big plate of fish, a pitcher of cold milk, cornbread, a bottle of ketchup, and off to the side, slices of watermelon.

After we'd finished and helped Grandmother clean up the table, we went out onto the front porch to sit in the swing. The locusts were humming. Lightning bugs were beginning to blink over by my grandmother's rose bushes. A rabbit slipped out of her iris bed and started munching on clover. We didn't say much . . . just sat there, watching the end of the day. I thought back about the river and the way it moved and how the fish lived in it.

Then I cocked my head. Something had stirred inside of me and whatever it was spread all through me. It was sort of like some kind of a compass released from its lock and held steady . . . now showing direction. And even though it was now very far away, and I'd cleaned up enough that Grandmother had let me come to the dinner table, I swear I could still smell that river. Somehow, someway, the river had gotten in my blood that day.

I'd been infected by Old River Chute with an incurable affliction. That was forty years ago and it's still in me. And I pray that I'll never be cured.

Bruins of the White River Bottoms

The flatbottom boat skimmed along the sandbar, throwing a wake that churned the shallows. The opposite bank, two hundred yards away, was high and steep, cut to bare earth by the force of the river. Where it met the water, the current swirled and sucked amid a tangle of logs, root wads, and ancient snags. Beyond both banks, silent, green, and magnificent, was the forest, dark and oozing mystery.

I was back home, with the forest and the river that had captured my heart when I was a boy more than thirty years earlier. It was here, in the lower reaches of the White River in Arkansas, that I'd heard the river sirens' call for the first time. I was fourteen years old when I heard it. The call became music that touched me in a way I'd never been touched before. Suddenly I was confronted by, actually enveloped by, something huge and powerful that worked as it was intended to work—a wild river, an awesome force, sculpturing the land, dictating its character, following the commands of seasons—and me, a thin boy only just beginning to resemble the man to come, following the commands of that river, guiding the raft I'd built, listening to the river speak to me, touched by the rawness of a place and a river left alone to be what it was intended to be. And I realized then that I too was doing what I was intended to do in the place where I was supposed to be.

In the decades that followed, my connection with that river and floodplain rivers in general had grown progressively stronger. Now I was an aging, grizzled, river fisheries professor on the faculty of the Department of Wildlife and Fisheries at Mississippi State University. The rivers talked to me in ways more powerful than ever before, in a language blending science and poetry and something beyond either. I was guided by these voices. I could shut my eyes and sense this river, the White, personified, a being, still strong but annoyed at the insults it had to endure from these insignificant creatures that came with their rapacious little tools, thinking that they could, in the end, prevail. The river laughed . . . a deep, dark laugh . . . and sucked at our boat, momentarily jerking it sideward and pulling at the stern, just to emphasize that the vision I had was not some fantasy but rather the ultimate reality. This river always wins in the end.

My spiritual connections to the river had been the basis for my invitation to be on it that day. I really wasn't there to be a scientist. Rather, I was there to transcend the disciplines of science, to move beyond hypothesis testing and measurements. I was there to listen, feel, share the messages, and provide a compass. With me was a young graduate student, Tom White, who was working on his Ph.D., studying black bears in the White River National Wildlife Refuge, and Bruce Leopold, his major professor.

As a fisheries biologist, I was the odd man on his doctoral dissertation research committee. The others were wildlife scientists and statisticians. I was the only one with webs between my toes, a fin on the nape of my neck, and scales under my armpits. Early in his tenure at the university Tom recognized river connections with his bears and river connections with me. After some long talks I accepted his invitation to join his doctoral committee and to come back to my old river haunts with him. The project was much more than a bear study. The bears were simply another way for the river to send its messages.

Tom was a natural river rat. He handled the boat with skill, cutting around snags, whisking along flats, cruising with the currents, reading the water, understanding the reality that faint messages on the surface can reflect big stuff below. It took less than an hour in the boat with him to realize that I was in good hands, that this was his world too.

I took a deep breath. The musty smell of dead gars mellowing out in the sun on a mud bar mingled with the dankness of vegetation living, dying, and rotting. Sunlight brushed the surface of the brown water, sparkling and flashing in our faces. A deer on one of the steep banks watched us approach, and, as we came near, it bounded back into the shadows. Turtles basking on snags plopped into the water. The outboard motor hummed. Wavelets hammered at the bottom of the boat. A pair of wood ducks jumped up from a quiet backwater and raced us to the next bend in the river before disappearing through the forest.

It was midafternoon, and our mission was to set several snares for bears before dark. Bears that we captured would be equipped with radio tags so that their movements could be tracked. With this information, Tom intended to write his dissertation about the way bears live in this wild land and how they relate to the dynamics of the river.

Tom slowed the boat and eased up to a big log jutting out into the current. I jumped out onto the log and tied the boat securely to it. Grabbing our packs, we all set out, first climbing the bank, then moving on through the forest searching for a bear trail. It wasn't long, perhaps twenty minutes or so, before we found what we were looking for. Bears are the ultimate creatures of habit. On their trails they set their feet exactly where they set them the last time they passed. The tracks were clear and distinct. We went to work.

First we cut brush and cane and made a sort of tepee that Tom called a "cubby." Then we secured a cable to a tree and made sure that it could revolve completely around the tree in a full circle without hitting another tree. Between the tree end and the free end of the cable was attached a heavy spring taken from the hood of an old car. This was to serve as the shock absorber. When a bear is captured, it runs hard and fast to the end of the cable, and there needed to be some "give" to prevent the bear from breaking a foot or leg. On the free end of the cable we prepared a noose with a one-way slip, and to this we attached a spring-loaded device with a trigger. Dead fish (carp and buffalo) were thrown into the cubby and brush was cut and placed as a funnel leading into the cubby's entrance. A log was placed across the entranceway and behind the log we put the spring-loaded noose. The bear would smell the fish, follow the easy entrance way to the log, step across the log, and bingo, we'd have our bear on a string.

By the time we'd finished the setup, we were covered with sweat and mosquito bites. Not a breath of wind stirred in the forest. Locusts hummed with the resonance that they have only on still, hot, late summer afternoons as the day begins to fade. It was time to go. We quickly surveyed our setup, gave it a stamp of approval, and hustled back to our boat. We had five more snares to set.

Three more sets were made along the crest of river bluffs along the main channel. Then we slipped back deep into the forest, following a tributary named Cuckleburr Bayou that twisted and turned and looped back on itself and occasionally spilled over into the surrounding bottomland hardwood forest. The main channel of the river is wild, but it is a highway. Back on that bayou, with trees hanging completely overhead, blocking the fading late afternoon sun, vines trailing into the brown stained water, backwaters extending back into shadows where cottonmouths lurked, herons standing like statues in shallow water areas . . . our way was transformed into an obscure path through what truly was the forest primeval.

If there is "wild" on this earth, then this world along Cuckleburr Bayou is it. Life oozed from the earth and water and especially where they mixed. Fish swirled as we moved slowly along against the bayou's slight current. This was the land that had led me into the mysteries of the wild as a boy. It was here that I'd stalk off on cloudy November days with shotgun and compass when I was in high school, drifting along cypress and tupelo gum breaks, following the course of twisting sloughs, hunting deer and squirrels and ducks. It was here that I'd drift with a boat, dipping minnows or crickets into brushy spots for crappie and bream. As Tom, Bruce, and I moved deeper into the forest, deeper into the wild, the soul and spirit of the river again reached out to stroke the soul and spirit of the man. There can be no more perfect union for me.

It took us longer to find bear sign along the bayou. There was no natural lay to the land, and so the bear trails couldn't be instinctively marked as they could be along the main channel of the river. But when we found sign, there was plenty of it and it was hot. This old bayou was command central for the bears.

We prepared two cubbies about a half mile apart, then drifted back down the bayou as shadows began to deepen with the evening hours. By the time we made it back out to the river, the sun was just brushing the tops of trees along the river channel. There was no wind, and so the surface of the water was slick and smooth. The reflections on the water from trees, the golden afterglow of the sun, and the clouds were magnificent. There was a chill to the air even though it was late July. Along the sandbars a slight mist was rising. The boat skimmed across the surface, smooth wake flowing in a "V" behind us, spreading, distorting reflections, and finally slipping across sandbars or bumping into bluffs.

Ahead were the bridge and the boat ramp. A small group of houseboats lay tethered along the river bank, some with lights on and others dark. We knew that one was really the residence of a commercial fisherman, while the others were more or less fishing and hunting camps, used only occasionally on weekends or during the hunting season. These people of the river were *my* people, linked to another rhythm, one of currents, mystery, and things wild and free. They in fact were wild and free people, only connected by tangents to the rules of the world and the society around them. And in actuality, they weren't really connected with that world at all, but rather bumped against it, and bounced off of it, seeking another way, not by choice but by virtue of some elemental difference in makeup, values, and methods of living. To those beyond the river and the wild lands through which it traced its currents, these people of the river were considered misfits, outlaws, anachronisms. To me, they were people of the dreamtime, beauty and rightness incarnate. And to them, and river people around the world, I'd dedicated my life, working to ensure that their way of life would endure through the ages, at least as long as I was on the pilgrimage, at least as long as I was blessed by breath, heartbeat, and a means to communicate.

We loaded the boat on the trailer and drove back in Tom's pickup truck to our camp, an old cabin down the road a piece. Once there we fried up some catfish and potatoes, warmed up some beans, uncapped bottles of cold beer and settled down to supper, serenaded by a chorus of green tree frogs, crickets, cicadas and chuck-will's-widows. We didn't talk much, but what little there was centered on bears, catfish, floods, and river people. Nothing else really mattered much.

There was a stillness outside . . . a deep midsummer southern night stillness that wraps itself around the world, thick, heavy, and somehow capable of touching deep within the soul of a man, letting him know that the world is in good shape, in good hands, that God is near. No need for "Taps." We hit our bunks full of catfish, full of peace, and full of anticipation of what our snares might produce in the morning. I slapped a couple of mosquitoes that had found their way through the screened windows and then drifted off into the land of the never-never.

Morning crept upon the river in ghost-like shrouds of swirling fog, drifting from the forest and moving low over the water. The river was dark. It seemed to suck at snags, causing them to bounce in the current. A big gar swirled. A couple of wood ducks skimmed the treetops on the opposite bank, the hen squealing to let us know that she had her man in tow. A snake dropped from its perch on a snag and, riding high (thus a cottonmouth), made its way to a logjam, no doubt in hopes that someone would come poking around the place so it could bite him later in the day.

Tom pumped up the gas line, adjusted the choke, and pulled a few times on the starter cord of the outboard motor. There was no response. He pumped the tank again, pushed the choke halfway in and pulled again. This time the outboard motor coughed, sputtered, and caught, sending a small cloud of blue smoke out behind the boat and into bubbles that popped to the surface. We let the motor warm for a few minutes to ensure that once we were out in the river, we wouldn't need to do any quick and fancy paddling to avoid a crash on that logjam where the cottonmouth was waiting. We knew that the old motor could be cantankerous first thing in the morning, like an old man getting lined out on his day. Once moving, however, it was dependable.

While the motor warmed, we put our equipment into the boat. If bears were caught, we had to take measurements, tissue samples, and blood. Then we had to put a radio collar on the beasts. All of this depended on giving the bear a good dose of "joy juice" to keep it sleepy for a while. We'd use a dart gun with hypodermic needle to deliver the prescribed dose of Telozol® based on the estimated weight of the critter. Too much and we'd have the ingredients for a bearskin rug. Too little, and, well . . . Arkansas bears can bite just like any other. The week before, one old bear had "come to" a bit before schedule, and Tom's assistant had had a merry time running around a big water oak tree as the bear tried to snatch him in the britches. We also packed water and lunch and I (not so secretly) packed my big .357 magnum revolver—not so much for bears but for "the unknown" which can reveal its ugly head in many and diverse forms in the wildwood bottoms of the Deep South's bigger rivers. Its presence tends to help discussions get to the point when you stumble across someone "farming in the woods." Short conversations and a sincere wish for all parties involved to say a quick goodbye are beneficial to the health of everyone.

Tom jumped into the driver's seat in front of the outboard, and gave the tank bulb a squeeze for good measure. Bruce took the middle seat, and I shoved us off into the swirling waters of the river. We moved slowly past the houseboats to avoid rocking their tethered boats and banging them against their moorings. Most, however, were already gone, as the owners were checking nets and lines.

Once past them, we forged ahead, anxious to check our snares and to process bears, if bears had been caught. We needed to set them free before the midday heat stressed them too much and before other bears found them. Snared bears tend to be at a serious disadvantage in the presence of other bears.

We went to the first set location, picked our way up the bank, and then moved into the woods quietly. We slowed as we approached the cubby, trying to see if there was a bear. We could see that the cubby was gone, torn to shambles. And we could see a bear lying stretched out on the ground, motionless. We eased up to it, and Tom tossed a stick at it. There was no movement. We moved closer and Tom poked it with a longer stick. The bear remained still. It was dead. We were too late. It had been killed by another bear.

The dead bear was a magnificent animal, slick, glossy black, in good condition. The marks on it didn't seem too severe and about the only thing that we could imagine was that it had overheated during its struggle and perhaps died of a heart attack or simply stress. Regardless, we were crestfallen. It was not our intention or our mission to cause mortality among the bears, but just the opposite—to ensure their survival on into future generations. We took a few measurements and a tissue sample from the bear, removed the snare, picked up our equipment and returned to the boat . . . sad, quiet, thoughtful. But we had to move on. We didn't want the situation repeated with other bears.

The next snare also had a bear. This one was alive, well, and kicking. Like the previous one, it had torn up the cubby and the area around the snare tree. It was still tumbling, rolling and biting at the cable that held it.

Tom estimated that it weighed about 150 pounds and measured out the tranquilizer for the dart gun. Slipping up close to the bear but beyond its reach, Tom took quick aim and popped the bear with the dart. The bear tore at the dart in its side with its teeth, but the chemical had already been delivered. Now we just waited.

After about three minutes the bear sat down and began panting. At five minutes, it lay down. At seven minutes, we walked up to it and Tom quickly wrapped strong duct tape around its mouth and put ointment in its eyes to protect them. He also put something on its nose that apparently masked our scent and thus would keep the incapacitated but very much awake bear at a lower stress level. Then we went to work, weighing the bear, drawing blood, taking a tooth, and placing a radio collar around its neck. By the time we'd done these things, the bear was beginning to stir. We moved our equipment back among the trees about forty yards from the bear and in dark shadows downwind. Then we rolled the bear onto its stomach and Tom unwrapped the tape around the bear's mouth. This done, we moved back to our equipment to wait. We'd have to watch the bear until it got up and walked away.

The bear slowly raised its head and began bobbing it slowly. It tried to sit but couldn't and so settled back down. Three or four minutes later, it tried again to sit and this time was able to. It just sat there, looking around, moving its old furry head from side to side, and then, suddenly, it was on its feet, swaying, trying to take a step. It would raise a front leg but then put it back down and rest. Then, slowly, it took a first step, then another and another and started moving off through the woods. From time to time, it would stop, as if getting its bearings, then move on for a few yards, stop again, and then move. After each stop, it seemed more sure footed and then, finally, it moved steadily out of our sight.

We had four more snares to check. The next two also had bears and we processed them as we had the first one. The third had a big male, and he was in the process of ripping up the place, rolling, biting at the snare cable around his foot, slapping at trees and trashing the cubby. Tom eased up for the shot with the dart gun and the bear lunged at him. Tom shot and the dart hit the bear in the hip. The bear immediately tore at the dart and it fell out. We waited for the drug to take affect but nothing seemed to be happening. So Tom loaded up again and delivered another shot, this time hitting the bear in the neck. The dart hung there, and we knew that this time we had the drug injected.

Five minutes later, Mr. Bear was on the ground with tape around his mouth and we were well on our way with processing him. When we finished, Tom said that he needed to move quickly to check the last snare because it was getting late in the morning. But I'd need to stay with the bear we'd just finished to make sure that he was O.K. and that no other bear attacked him while he was drugged and vulnerable. I asked Tom if he and Bruce could process a bear without my help and he said yes. So, as they moved back toward our boat, I settled down in the shadows to watch the big male recover. Apparently the first shot had delivered some of its juice, because it seemed to take forever for him to lift his head. It was a full thirty minutes before the bear was sitting up on his haunches and more than an hour before he lumbered off into the woods, weaving like some drunk on a Saturday night down a street in nearby Dumas.

But as I waited for his recovery, as I sat watching, feeling, listening, searching through mind and soul, I was enveloped once again by the spirit of the forest. The heat was rising and all was quiet. There was no wind. Nothing stirred except an occasional prothonotary warbler down along a nearby slough. The quiet was awesome. The huge trees were like pillars in some cathedral. The bear, dark and glistening before me, was a catalyst that opened pathways into dimensions of primordial reflections, a linkage timeless, without boundaries, transforming me into someone else, something else, that I knew to be the ageless oversoul of humankind.

I was enraptured by a vision. I saw that this was the world to which we would return eventually. After all our trappings, after all our attempts to live separated from this world of rivers, forests, floods, seasons, and great beasts, we would come home. I felt the presence of God very near as the bear turned his head and looked at me. I knew that he saw me. We just stared at each other for a while, clearing away our respective fogs, reconnecting with the earth, each in our own way.

Then, in the distance, I could hear the whining of the outboard motor and knew that Tom and Bruce were on their way to pick me up. The bear heard it also, turned his head toward the sound and then back toward me. Then he got up, shaky but with deliberation, and walked back to the path he'd been traveling when lured by the smell of fish to the cubby and the snare.

I too got up, also a bit shaky but with deliberation, and walked back to the river where Tom was in the process of securing the boat. I asked him if he'd caught a bear. He said yes, a small female and that she was doing fine.

"How'd your bear do?" he asked.

"It took a while, but he'll be O.K.," I answered as I took my seat in the front of the boat. But unlike the bear, the snare which held *me* would never be released. I was to be forever connected with this land and the river. And, unlike the bear, I didn't particularly want to tug too hard.

Jungle Gold

The old man's eyes shone in the soft glow of the lantern. Beyond the thin walls of the hut the jungle was pulsing with sound. There was a ceaseless resonating whine of insects that merged with the shrill calls of tree frogs. Night birds whooped and tonked from deep amid the shadows. Yet with all the noise, all the vibrant pulsing of life oozing from the forest, there was a sense of quiet that enveloped us as the old man spoke of his days and adventures as a fisherman on the Pahang River.

The Pahang River courses through the very heart of the oldest forest in the world, and is the last and longest undisturbed river in peninsula Malaysia. Elephant, tiger, leopard, gaur, sambar deer, and rhino can be found in the region. Mornings reverberate with the calls of gibbons and the crash of leaf monkeys as they move through the jungle canopy. Hornbills fly along the edge where river and jungle meet. There are occasional camps along the river and scattered throughout the jungle that are made by the orang asli (aboriginal people). These are the "dream people," the nomadic forest wanderers.

As a nomadic forest wanderer myself, I could identify well with the orang asli. For twenty years I'd known them and their world. I'd first come to Malaysia in the late 1970s as a U.S. Peace Corps volunteer, and during my two-year tour I'd traveled deep into the jungle and lived in the remote kampongs (villages). I learned to speak Malay in order to teach my courses at the National University of Malaysia, and although the orang asli had other languages, most could understand and speak Malay. In the course of the following two decades, I'd returned to Malaysia many times to reconnect and strengthen my bonds with the land and the people that owned such a large chunk of my heart. On this particular trip, I'd invited one of my recent doctoral graduates, John Jackson (no relation) to accompany me. He'd conducted river fisheries research with me as my compadre for many years in the southeastern U.S. and had done fine work. When he got his Ph.D., I'd offered him a trip to Southeast Asia and he'd jumped at the chance.

On this night full of mystery and enchantment the old fisherman shared his stories with me and I translated them for John. The old fisherman spoke the languages that were our common bonds, the verbal Malay and the spiritual songs of the river. He'd been hesitant at first to speak, not knowing how well I understood these languages. Through the ages river people around the world have learned that most people cannot understand what they're trying to say. But, with reassurance from the federal game warden accompanying us, the old fisherman began. When he paused, I'd reflect on what he'd said. Soon he realized that he could tell his tale.

"The river has its own life, its own way," he said. "We must respect it, not fight it. If we do this, it will share its treasures. If we do not, then we will be forced into battles that we will lose."

He told of the spirits that lurked in the murky depths of the river's lower reaches. They came in the form of huge catfish that could destroy boats and kill men. Most, however, had left the river now that the national park had improved visitor access and accommodation. Most of the park visitors did not hear the voice of the river, and they paid people to capture the spirit fish so that they could eat them. In fact, he himself had done this in order to earn money. But before the new park developments, there was no money for fish. Fish were caught only when the fisherman, his family, or kampong needed fish to eat. But sometimes he caught fish to trade with other kampongs for the meat of wild deer.

As the night deepened he spoke of boat building and of capture techniques and of the wild places where people rarely went. In this last regard, he mentioned a special day and a special fish. In the upper reaches of the Tembling River, he'd once put a frog on a hook and let the hook drift into the tea-stained water below a jumble of boulders. As the frog went past the rocks, he jerked his line and a fish had struck with awesome force. When he pulled back, the fish jumped high into the air. The sunlight had glistened from golden scales. The water sparkled. The river was happy to show its treasure. He was happy to receive it in so fine a fashion. The name of the fish? Sebarau.

I asked if there were more sebarau in the river and he said yes, there were many, but to go to where they were would mean many days of travel and a guide would be necessary.

With this last statement, he looked directly at me and we both grinned. No firmer contract had ever been established by two men.

The next morning we loaded two river canoes with fuel and supplies to last a week and hired three more men to help us with the trip. By late morning we were ready to depart. Prayers were said and the outboard motors on the backs of the canoes were cranked. We shoved the bows out into the current and were on our way in search of sebarau.

The river boiled and surged around us as we made our way upstream. Although it was a lowland stream with a large forested floodplain, there were still sections that cut close to mountains, and in these places, there were rock cliffs along the river banks and large boulders out in the stream. As the hours passed the frequency of orang asli camps along the river declined rapidly. Soon there were none at all. The murkiness of the water also declined and became more tea colored. The trees began to reach across the stream, trying to link with those on the opposite banks. Vines trailed in the current. Water swirled around exposed roots and old logs near the shore. There were occasional splashes as some creature, usually a snake or turtle, plopped into the river after spotting us. Deer and wild pigs crashed through the brush. Parrots, hornbills, barbets, and leaf birds filled the air with color and bright patterns. Butterflies drifted through the shadows and tiny sunlit spots, adding a surreal dimension of enchantment to the afternoon as it deepened.

I was enveloped by the jungle's closeness, the green blanket that surrounded me. I was enraptured by the river, the thread of life flowing beside, beyond, and somehow within me. I entered into a different realm of being, the one that forever draws me out into the wild and lonely places, the one that opens my heart and soul, the one that quickens my mind, the one that stops the clock. I was no longer the university professor, bound by desk, telephone, meetings, and administrative tasks, no longer the suburban man, bounded by shopping malls, stoplights, restaurants, and civic responsibilities. I was transformed into that other person who lurks deep within my oversoul. He only comes out when my internal dialogue is stilled by the power of wild places. Wild rivers nearly always release him, as do also mountains, glaciers, deserts, and deep swamps. But it takes time.

John noticed the transformation at the end of our first day and mentioned it to me. We were sitting on a grassy spot near the river, with wild bees crawling all over us, licking salt (they won't sting unless you slap at them). The sky was the deepest of blues. The stream bank on the opposite side of the river was vibrant with butterflies and small birds. Our canoes were tethered. The men who were with us were setting up our camp in an old hut, boiling tea and cooking rice over a fire. The jungle rustled with life. Hawks soared among the clouds. A white-handed gibbon sat perched on a branch, quietly watching us.

"Dr. Jackson," he said, "something has happened to you today. You're somebody different. I'm not sure I know who you are now but I think you belong here."

Then he paused, sighed, and said, "Well, I finally found it."

"Found what?" I asked.

"Paradise."

I could only smile and nod. There is something about tropical Asia that touches me in a way no other part of the world can. The shades of green seem deeper here than anywhere else. The pastel colors of the sunsets seem richer. The sounds from the forest, the sea, even the cities, seem to penetrate deeper into my heart. The spirit of the land seems to enter deeper into my soul. It is a land where I've experienced my greatest happiness and my greatest sadness. It is a land that has carried me into the dream time and one that has on other occasions crushed my dreams. I've found no middle ground in Malaysia. When I leave Malaysia, a piece of my heart always remains there.

There was no way that I could explain this to John. But he sensed the power of this ancient land with its primeval forest and eternal rivers. Perhaps with time, a piece of his heart would also belong to Asia.

The old fisherman called to us. It was time to eat supper.

Sitting on the floor, the firelight casting its light on the dark wall of the jungle around us, we ate in silence. The rice was served on washed wild banana leaves. A curry of fish and peppers and unknown spices was added to it along with a handful of peanuts. We ate with our hands in typical Malay fashion, savoring the wonderful flavors, made especially so by the seasoning of the day's trip up the river and the splendor of a tropical night unfolding above us.

The night was so clear. Earlier that afternoon, there had been heavy rain. It happens almost every day here in this part of Malaysia. Then it cleared at sunset, leaving the air washed, cool and fresh. Now, with the cleansed air, the stars began to pop out in the ever-darkening sky. Nightjars began to fill the air with their calls. The insects started their humming. Water dripped off branches and leaves. There was a sharp bark from somewhere back in the jungle, and one of the men warned us not to venture beyond the edge of the fire's light. The bark had been from a deer that apparently had been taken by a tiger or leopard. It was indeed a "tiger" night. Wet, dripping, quiet . . . I'd learned of them through my previous years in this tropical world. Tigers love such nights. They hunt especially well under these conditions.

The next morning I got up early and decided to explore the river bank before we broke camp. The morning was pleasantly cool, but I decided that I really didn't need to dress much. So, I put on only a light pair of cotton shorts, a shirt, and some old jungle boots.

There was a trail along the river. I followed it. There were prints of tapir, deer, and wild pig. Overhead, monkeys cavorted among the branches. In the distance I heard the crowing of jungle fowl. I pushed farther and farther along the trail for perhaps an hour and then heard a soft rumbling.

I froze. The rumbling came again from beyond a jumbled pile of limbs perhaps sixty feet ahead of me. There could be only two sources of that sound—tiger or leopard. I took a step backward, knowing that tigers tend to attack from behind. If they see your face, at least so the sayings go, they will not charge. As for leopards, I had no idea. But as slowly and as deliberately as possible, I stepped backward and just as slowly I peeled off my white cotton shirt. If there was an attack, I had no weapon and could only perhaps distract attention by throwing a white shirt away from me. I could think of nothing else to do.

The rumbling came again, but I continued my backward walk. After about fifty yards, I turned and walked another fifty yards, then I ran like a scoundrel for several hundred yards along that river bank trail.

The only thing that I could think of was that I'd encountered a big cat on its kill. It didn't want to kill again but was ready to defend what it already had. When I backed away, that was all the cat wanted.

Breakfast was waiting when I got back to camp. Over tea, rice and eggs I recounted my experience on the trail. The others listened solemnly, especially the old fisherman, but said nothing. This was the Malaysian jungle. Things in it bite. No need to say anything.

After breakfast, we broke camp, loaded up the canoes, and were on our way again. We motored upstream perhaps two or three hours, then stopped while one of the men in the other canoe went up on the river's bank to explore. He returned with some fruit about the size of a Ping-Pong ball and we were on our way. The old fisherman said they were bait.

A few minutes later we stopped to fish. One of the fruits was placed on a hook and a few of the others were thrown into the water, making a plopping sound. From around the pool we could see the movements of fish as they moved toward the plopping sound. We waited and waited but there were no bites. After about an hour of trying, we left. The fish we'd tried to get were not sebarau but rather fruit-eating fish that would have been our evening meal had we captured some.

However, I have an image permanently etched into my mind of one of the men fishing for those fish. He was sitting on the smooth stones of a gravel bar, motionless, waiting for a fish to bite the fruit on the end of his line. He seemed to blend into the surrounding environment, one with the forest and the river, yet poised to strike given the opportunity. His focus never drifted from the line. He was like a leopard, relaxed but ready in an instant to pounce on his prey. But, as is true for the leopard, there are many hunts that yield nothing. Finally giving up, he returned to the boat and got in. There was no comment. The world just is as the world is. And we were gone.

Upstream, beyond that fishing hole, the river became much smaller and its current much faster. The distinction between rapids and pools was much more distinct. There were shallow spots that required us to get out of the canoes and push them on into deeper water. Along the shore there was more evidence of elephants. They ripped branches from trees in their foraging and had crossing spots that were apparently used regularly. These spots were dappled with their dung.

From time to time we encountered large trees that had fallen across the river. In some cases, they had barely missed making it completely to the other side of the 150-foot-wide river channel. We were able to make it around all of them until late that afternoon. It was then that we encountered a monarch of a tree that had made it completely across, blocking any further upstream travel in our canoes.

We accepted the reality of the situation, but I asked the old fisherman if there were sebarau in these waters. He grinned and said that we'd been in "sebarau water" since leaving camp that morning and did I want to *see* one. It was obvious that he had emphasized the word "see" and had not used the word "catch."

I said that I was ready to see one and he began talking with the man who had been unsuccessful fishing earlier. The man rigged up heavy-duty spinning tackle and tied a very large metal silver spoon lure to his line. Then we began drifting downstream, the man casting as we went.

He was an expert, actually more an artist, at casting. He was able to put that spoon into tiny pockets around stumps, roots, and boulders and then retrieve rapidly, keeping the lure in full motion even as we drifted toward it. After about fifteen minutes, there was a terrific strike. A fish weighing perhaps five pounds jumped clear of the water, shook its head, and threw the spoon right back at us.

We drifter farther down the river, past rocks and roots, into an area with deep water and swirls. The fisherman worked the water carefully. After another fifteen or twenty minutes, there was another heavy strike and this time the man set the hook hard. As with the previous fish, the sebarau jumped high out of the water, shaking its head. But this time the hook held, and the fish went ripping down the river with us in hot pursuit.

It jumped at least four or five more times, each time ripping line from the spinning reel and forcing us to chase it as it tore downstream. By the time the fish was brought into the boat we'd traveled perhaps half a mile down the river. It was an incredible fight and one that proclaimed not only the status of the sebarau as an excellent sport fish but also the status of the man as an accomplished fisherman in his own right. With the fish in the boat, he grinned. The old fisherman had given the man a chance to save face and the man had been able to do so.

The old fisherman handed the fish to me for inspection. It weighed about ten pounds and was a beautiful golden color with a black bar across its side. It was a kind of carp but it was shaped like a bass, with all of the predatory features, including behavior, of a bass. It had large, powerful fins and its tail was thick and well muscled. Its entire body was sleek and tapered somewhat like a high-backed torpedo, seemingly made to order for explosive attacks and hard-charging runs.

After I'd looked over the fish and taken some photographs, the old fisherman indicated that it was time for more fishing. He handed the rod to me. It was heavy and, for me, not a very well-balanced rig. I cast poorly with it at first but after an hour or so was able to do O.K. The heavy spoon required some fast reeling since the boat was constantly moving downstream in the direction of the cast. We didn't cast upstream behind the boat because to do so would risk getting the hook snagged and subsequently necessitate trying to turn the boat around in the narrow channel to save the lure. Also, the sebarau would have been alerted by the boat passing.

I cast and I cast but with no results. Finally, I had a strike and felt a fish on the line. It peeled off about twenty feet of line, jumped, and threw the lure back at me. I quickly reeled in and kept on fishing. But that encounter with the sebarau was my one and only.

The old fisherman finally suggested that I pass the rod back to the other man, and I followed his instructions. A half an hour later, there was another sebarau of about three pounds in the boat and the old fisherman said that was enough for supper. We cranked the outboards and set out to beat the sunset back to our old camp of the previous night.

The Malays built a fire behind the old campsite, organized their gear, and then, as the fire mellowed for cooking, they drifted off to say their evening prayers. John and I drifted back the other direction, toward the river, allowing the coming night to weave its threads of mystery and beauty around us. Nightjars "tonked" from some hidden place across the river. We could hear the water around the rocks. Faintly we could hear the stirring of the men at prayer, then heard them returning to camp and the fire.

There was a gentle call from the old fisherman. "Encik, ada siap maken emas yang datang daripada sungai kita kah?" ("Sir, are you ready to eat the gold that came from our river?")

And I answered, "Kalau kami makan bersama sama emas itu akan membuat kami semua adik laki-laki." ("If we eat this gold together we will become brothers.")

To this he grinned and said, "Kami sudah ada ber-laki-laki di sungai. Mari, kita makan." ("We're already brothers of the river. Come, let us eat.")

The power of gold is beyond imagining, but the power of a river overwhelms it.

Swamp Slogging

In the predawn darkness Don Flynn and I pulled on our hip boots and grabbed our shotguns from the back seat of my father's car. From the trunk I hoisted an old army duffle bag with our six decoys and slung it on my shoulder. With all of our stuff we set off down the road to the head of a trail leading back through the swamp to our duck hole.

The morning was frosty but not cold. There was a sweetness to the still air that only occurs on Saturday mornings in December for sixteen-year-old boys going duck hunting. Stars winked at us through the bare branches of the trees alongside the road. In the quietness, the hoot of an owl seemed to echo through the woods. The water on either side of the road was dark and inky looking.

This was a new adventure for us. Don Flynn and I had hunted together for a couple of years and had been driving for nearly a year. But this was our first duck season, in fact our first duck hunt, when we'd been given permission to drive alone. We had to be back by 9:30 that morning, because my father, a Protestant minister in one of the community's churches, needed his car to get to the church to finish working on his sermon for the following day. Time wouldn't permit us to range out to hunt the minnow ponds twenty miles from town, nor a family friend's rice reservoir an hour away, or even the little creek at Mr. Cartmel's farm the other side of the air force base where we'd first discovered the magic of whistling wings over decoys.

We were sort of caught. We cherished the independence of being able to drive alone. And we were totally consumed with duck hunting. All we talked about were guns, loads, decoys, calls, boats, and boots. We wanted to be in the wide, wild, and lonely places where the sky would be full of mallards, or hunkered down in the bushes on the banks of rice reservoirs or minnow ponds where teal and bluebills would come busting across the levees like fighter jets. But our tight schedule dictated a shorter range.

So, on the previous Wednesday afternoon, between the time school let out and our Explorer Boy Scout troop meeting that night, we'd slipped away in my family's car to scout out a tiny tupelo gum swamp located about two miles from my house. The whole swamp probably wasn't more than 150 acres, and a highway ran right down through the middle of the thing. We'd never been in the swamp before. However, a friend of ours had told us of hunting fox squirrels on the west side of the highway along the edge of the swamp, and that he'd seen a few ducks from time to time. But although he also hunted ducks (mostly in a creek near his house), he'd never actually been out in the swamp to hunt ducks.

From our perspective, it seemed that the east side of the swamp might be a better place for us. For one thing, our friend did not hunt there and so we wouldn't be bothering him. But mostly it seemed that the east side was bigger and wilder. We dropped a lot of hints around trying to find out something about the place, but we couldn't seem to find anyone who had ever been in that part of the swamp. Subsequently, we had no idea about how deep the water might be (and whether we might need a boat) or whether or not there really was anything in it to hunt. The mystery of the place was a powerful lure.

Our Wednesday afternoon scouting mission was done more from the attitude of spies or perhaps as an army reconnaissance team than as hunters. In fact, we didn't even carry our shotguns. In their place we had small backpacks with pieces of aluminum foil, a few nails, and hammers. Our idea was to mark a trail that we could find in the darkness of the upcoming Saturday morning hunt.

Slowly we moved through the dark water, tacking up a piece of foil every fifty feet or so. After we were about two hundred yards back away from the road, the brush cleared, and we found ourselves in a sort of natural cathedral. The gum trees shot straight up from the water and then formed arches over our heads. The late afternoon sun cast golden rays through the watery forest, giving the whole place an ethereal aura. We were spellbound, silent, looking around and at each other. The reflections on the water shimmered. The green moss on the tree trunks and the smell of swamp gas that bubbled up from our boots when we stepped convinced us that we'd stumbled onto a remnant of the forest primeval.

We stood there quietly, listening to the pileated woodpeckers and the barking of fox squirrels. Nuthatches worked the tree trunks and wrens worked the fallen logs. On some of the larger logs we could see sign of raccoons. From time to time a big fish swirled. I don't think we would have been very surprised if after one of those swirls the head of a dinosaur had poked up. Somehow, and for whatever reason, this place had been bypassed by the forces of human civilization and development; it was a tiny jewel in a clutter of brick, asphalt, and steel. And somehow the swamp was able to buffer even the noise of the "other world." We could barely hear the sounds of vehicles on the highway. But we *could* hear the sounds of stiff wings whistling overhead.

By then it was starting to get dusky dark, and we realized that we had to start back to the car or we'd be late for supper and our scout meeting. The trouble was that we'd only marked the trail coming in and had not even thought of marking a return trail with foil on the opposite sides of the trees. Although just a little way into the swamp, we realized that we were in a pretty wild place. Getting back out took us about a half an hour longer than had the trip into the duck hole. But that just poured fuel onto the fire of our duck hunter hearts. During the whole time in the swamp we found absolutely no evidence that anyone else had been in there. It therefore was "ours," our own special duck hole. We'd heard ducks even though we had not seen any, but that had been enough for us. Saturday morning was an eternity away.

Now with eternity behind us, we cast our flashlights back into the woods straining for a reflection that would put us on the trail to our duck hole. But somehow that aluminum foil didn't seem to shine very well, and even after we found our first mark, it was tough going in the dark, sloshing through the water, hauling our decoy bag up and over the logs and stumps. We found also that stump holes had somehow been formed since we'd left the swamp on Wednesday, and we both managed to step into one that put water over the top of our boots. Pushing on, we realized that we'd miscalculated the amount of time it would take us to get to the place where we had planned to hunt. The sky turned from black to grey, and suddenly we had wood ducks landing all around us.

Although we didn't know it then, decoys really aren't necessary to attract wood ducks early in the morning. All you have to do is stand in the shadows and slosh water. We'd been doing a pretty good job of this all the way in from the road. Now, with unloaded guns and still not to our shooting spot, we were covered up with ducks.

Flynn started loading his gun. I took the cue and quickly slipped the decoy bag from my shoulder to load my own gun. More ducks poured by overhead and Flynn shot one. Suddenly the sky was full of ducks, as if every wood duck in the county had roosted there in that little swamp. That, in fact, was pretty much the truth as we later found out.

Hurriedly, I dumped the decoys out of the bag and began throwing them out. I don't think they were needed, but I was determined to hunt ducks the "proper" way. No sooner had the decoys plopped in the water than another big bunch of wood ducks fell in through the tree tops, whistling and squealing, coming in as if they'd never ever seen a human being standing in the water by a gum tree. I shot and killed a drake and Flynn also knocked one down. Then another flock came in and we both shot. One more duck fell. That sobered us up because now we had our limit of four wood ducks. We could shoot at other ducks but not anymore at wood ducks.

For about a half an hour the wood ducks worked over that swamp and we just stood there awestruck. How could it be that we were in this place all by ourselves? People all over Arkansas were driving hundreds of miles to get this kind of duck hunting and here we were just beyond the city limits of North Little Rock, covered up with ducks and with absolutely no competition. Wood ducks were flying and swimming everywhere. After the shooting stopped they actually became very tame. They swam among our decoys and between

Flynn and me. They chased each other around, bobbing their heads and squealing and splashing water over their backs. The morning sun glistened on the crests of the drakes. The hens dipped their beaks around the edges of fallen trunks where duckweed and acorns had been concentrated either by wind or by some current through the swamp.

We stayed in our duck shooting hole until 8:30, hoping for other kinds of ducks, and especially for mallards, but none came. This was wood duck territory, we were to learn. But as wood duck territory, it was the finest, and it would become the backbone, the foundation, of our duck hunting in the years to come.

We had our limit of four wood ducks, and we knew that we would have to get back home on time with my dad's car or run the risk of losing our driving privileges for future Saturday morning hunts. So we gathered up the decoys and slogged back out to the road. Once back to the road we hid our guns, decoys, and ducks and quickly walked to the car. We didn't want anyone driving by to see a couple of high school boys with all the evidence of a successful duck hunt. We drove past the stash to the other end of the swamp road, turned around, made sure we were not being tailed by another car, and when we were near our gear, I slowed down and Flynn grabbed the stuff and threw it into the back seat. We made it home with fifteen minutes to spare, a wet back seat, and big grins on our faces. The hardest thing would be to keep the secret to ourselves and the grins off our faces when we went back to school the following

Monday morning. But, except for sharing the place with close friends in our Explorer Boy Scout troop, we managed to keep the swamp secret for the remaining time we were in high school.

During those high school years there would be other duck hunts in other places, but always that swamp was there beckoning. Our parents liked it a lot because it kept us close most of the time and they knew that we'd be back home by midmorning when we hunted there. We liked it because it truly was "ours." In all the times I hunted it, only once did I ever see another person in the swamp other than the boys in our Explorer Boy Scout troop that hunted with Don and me. On that one occasion I saw an elderly black gentleman hunting with a small boy, perhaps his grandson, around the edges of the water for squirrels, not ducks.

And then there were the special days . . .

It is said that most hunters go through stages that include "the shooter," "the competitor," "the expert," "the specialist," and "the sportsman." Sometimes stages are skipped and sometimes they get jumbled together. Sometimes a hunter gets hung up in one of the stages and just doesn't move beyond it. To a very large degree, the swamp was where I passed through my evolutionary stages as a hunter, but they were somewhat different from the ones listed above.

I passed through the shooter stage fairly quickly, but during those early two or three years, I thought I hadn't been hunting unless I'd shot up at least one box of shells and preferably more. If game wasn't cooperating, I'd shoot at blackbirds and meadowlarks or even dirt clods and old cans—anything to avoid the shame of coming home with shells still in my pocket. Unless a boy has access to some sort of shooting club where he can practice on clay pigeons, he must shoot at other things if he is ever to learn about shotgunning. After a couple of years, however, things sort of get worked out in the young hunter's mind, and some sort of switch comes on that gets the coordination in working order. This is good for nongame wildlife, good for the pocketbook, and does wonders for a nonathletic boy's sense of self-worth. He knows in his heart that he can hit a flying duck and that's really all that counts. Let others make tackles and touchdowns, win races, and smash home runs. He's a hunter and can hit what he shoots at.

When the boy knows this, there's another switch that also clicks on. He realizes that he doesn't have to take every shot that comes by. This happened to me one cloudy, green-gray January morning out in the swamp. And it caused me to skip a stage or two in the hunter's evolutionary process.

Don Flynn and I had hunted wood ducks early that morning just like we had every morning during that Christmas holiday. There were not a whole lot of ducks, but some had come in and we'd killed one apiece. Then there was sort of a lull, with no ducks flying at all.

I got restless and told Don that I was going to wander around a bit and hunt fox squirrels. It was a very still day with a storm pending, and the fox squirrels had been active most of the morning. We rarely if ever hunted them in the swamp, because usually we went to the swamp for ducks and down to my uncle's farm in Lonoke or to a wildlife management area near Hazen for squirrels.

I had number six shot in the gun and a double handful of the shells in my hunting coat pocket. I hadn't gone fifty yards when I saw the first squirrel. He was a big fellow, all puffed up in his winter fur and standing out like a big orange ball on the gray branch. Using all of my dryland squirrel hunting stealth, I eased up to him and popped him. In the process I marveled at how quiet I had been able to be during the stalk. By moving slowly through the knee-to-thigh-deep water, I hardly made a ripple and also there was absolutely no noise.

In another fifteen minutes, I had three more squirrels. I'd killed a single and then, a few minutes later, a pair in a classic double shot. I almost lost one of the pair, however, because it landed in water a bit deeper than the others and I had a hard time spotting its tail floating submerged under the surface. Now that I had four squirrels in my game pouch in less than half an hour, something started to bother me. Something wasn't right. Then I saw another squirrel and stalked up to it just like I'd been able to do with the others. The squirrel had no idea that I was there . . . no ripples, no noise. I took a careful aim, put the bead of the shotgun barrel on that squirrel, slipped off the safety, and couldn't shoot. This wasn't right. I knew I wasn't *that* good a squirrel hunter.

I put the safety back on my shotgun, stepped out of the shadows beside the tree and spoke to that squirrel. For a few moments he just stared at me as I talked. I told him that he needed to look at the water as well as the sky and that hawks were not the only thing that could get him in the swamp. It didn't take long for that message to sink in to Mr. Squirrel's head and he skuttled around to the backside of the gum tree. I walked away from him and out to a patch of dry land beside the swamp. There was something strangely warm inside of me that I'd never felt before. I didn't want that feeling to go away, but after about twenty minutes it did.

As I walked along the edge of the swamp I noticed that the wind was starting to blow ever so slightly. I thought that would be good for Don, because it would make the decoys move and maybe he would be able to get another duck if they did. Then I heard a whistling of wings and a hen wood duck came ripping by over the treetops. I swung up on her instinctively, shot, and down she came. That warm feeling I'd lost came back to me and it confused me. It had come when I chose *not* to shoot the fox squirrel, and it had come to me when I'd just shot a duck. I went over to pick up my duck, and as I did the kinks worked themselves out in the equation. There's hunting and there's killing and there's a fine line between the two. That morning, shooting fox squirrels had been so easy that it was really mostly killing, but swinging on that fast-flying duck and making a good shot on her after wishing silently to myself that my buddy was going to get some shooting was hunting. Thirty-five years later I still *hunt* squirrels and ducks but I haven't *killed* any for a very long time.

As hard as I tried, I couldn't read the note scratched on the scrap of paper and placed in the window of Don Flynn's bedroom. It was 5:00 a.m. and we had our Saturday morning duck hunt scheduled. Typically, I'd get to his house a little early, tap on his bedroom window, and he'd be out to meet me carrying a glass of milk and his shotgun within ten minutes. He'd never before left a note in the window, but when I saw it I figured it said he wasn't going to be duck hunting that morning. Unlike the rest of the boys in the old Explorer Boy Scout troop, Don had a *real* girlfriend, and, given that he had his driver's license and that there was some classy play over across the river in Little Rock, I suspected he'd been out until really late Friday night. So I didn't keep on tapping. Some things—not many but some—*are* more important than duck hunting for a seventeen-year-old boy.

I drove on out to the swamp and parked my dad's car in the graveled spot just off the road. For some reason the highway department (or so I assumed) had thrown a bit of gravel on the place after our first season of duck hunting in the swamp. In later years I began to figure out that our "secret" place really wasn't much of a secret among the adults in the community who raised us. Mysterious things like gravel dumped in the right place, or a new box of shotgun shells tucked away on the blind side of the car and discovered after a hunt, just seemed to happen.

It was the first time I'd ever hunted the swamp alone. In fact, I wasn't sure that I was *allowed* to hunt the swamp alone. But in the predawn hours of a Saturday morning with my heart set on a duck hunt, I figured it would be easier to ask forgiveness than to ask permission.

Even so, I felt pretty weird walking down the road without Don Flynn, and finally decided that I wouldn't hunt in our old duck hole. That duck hole was "ours," not "mine." So I left the road on the other side and went into a sector we'd never hunted and with which I was totally unfamiliar.

It was pretty brushy for the first hundred yards or so, just like the other side, but unlike the other side, it did not have the big tupelo gum trees making a cathedral. Rather, the area was an aggregate of open spots around which grew some pretty large cypress trees and water oaks. The holes were not deep, however, and never did the water get much over knee deep. I chose one of the holes and scattered my decoys out in the middle of it. Then I backed up to one of the big oaks and pulled out my duck call.

I do not know why I pulled out that duck call. The swamp was a wood duck place, not a mallard place. Wood ducks do not come to a call. They come to splashing water and decoys in the shadows of early morning. Mallards come to calls and tend to prefer flying later in the morning. But I puffed a little air through the call and then blew a highball call followed by a bit of chuckling. I kicked the water some, but not much. The day dawned and I saw only a few ducks, and these were headed to our old duck hole across the road. I stayed where I was, watching ice form a skim around the open area where I had the decoys and occasionally shifting my weight to keep my toes from growing cold and numb. Then I heard a quack. Wood ducks don't quack.

I longed to look up but knew better than to do that. Nothing will flare a duck like the bright shiny face of a duck hunter. So I tucked my chin, kept the call to my mouth, and started a feeding call chuckle. I could hear the whistle of wings as the ducks circled, and, when they passed over my open area where I had my decoys spread out, I could see their reflection: mallards!

They circled twice, then locked their wings. There were three of them, two drakes and a hen. I could hardly believe what was happening but knew I had to be careful. Duck numbers in North America were at an all-time low and the limit on mallards was one duck. I could not afford a shot that might accidently kill two of them. They were so close together as they floated through the air, seemingly hanging there for an eternity, and then one of the drakes veered to the left. This was my chance!

I swung on him, shoved the end of the gun barrel just a little ahead of his yellow beak, and shot. He came down with a loud plop and started swimming around in crazy circles with his head under the water. Then he was still. But I wasn't. I was shaking all over, trembling so hard that I could not reload my gun.

"A mallard!" I thought. "A mallard from the swamp! And I did it all alone!"

I just couldn't believe it as I walked out to pick him up. He was so beautiful. His green head shone almost as if it were iridescent blue. It was that dark. His breast was a gorgeous chestnut. His sides were sleek and grey. His feet were bright orange and his beak was a wonderful yellow. And he had those all-important curly tail feathers that all duck hunters need to put on their hunting hats and cram into the space between cloth and trimming near the car's (or preferably pickup truck's) rearview mirror. As gently as I could, so as not to ruffle his feathers, I carried him back to the base of the big oak where I'd been standing and laid him out on a log. I didn't want my trophy to get all wet and soggy.

By that time I'd settled down (some) and was able to reload my gun. But it was so hard to look out at the sky and the woods. My eyes kept drifting toward that old bull mallard. It wasn't until I heard the squeal and the rush of wings that I realized that I was in the duck hunting business again. I looked up and there was a pair of wood ducks just about to settle into my decoys.

My gun was to my shoulder and one of the ducks was falling from the sky before I consciously realized that I was shooting. Then I swung on the second duck and it came down too! A double! How can a boy live with such a morning: not only a drake mallard but also a double on wood ducks!

I had the limit of three ducks on my hands and a pounding heart in my chest. There were three shotgun shells floating in the water next to the oak. The sun was just breaking through the trees. Ice had almost covered the open area in front of me and had already formed little shields around each of my decoys. It was only then that I realized that I was cold.

I carefully put my unloaded shotgun on the log beside my ducks, making sure that it was wedged in between a couple of limbs so that it wouldn't slip into the water, and with gloveless hands, got my decoys, wrapped their weight lines around their necks, stuffed them into the frozen-stiff army duffle bag, strung my ducks, slung ducks and bag across my shoulders, and sloshed my way out of the flooded woods. I think that was the very first time in my life that I felt like I was really a grown man. I was seventeen years old on my way home from a solo duck hunt. I'd killed a limit of ducks, including a mallard I'd called in myself and a double on wood ducks. The load on my back felt good. I liked the weight. The gun felt light and the hip boots were not heavy. The cold air stung my cheeks. My hands were red and raw. And, as I recall, there was a "whoop" that echoed through that woods as I made the last fifty yards back to the road.

There is an old dusty drake wood duck hanging on the wall over my bed. By today's taxidermy standards, it is a pretty mediocre mounting job. But thirty-five years ago it was considered a first-class piece of work. Now, I must accept what it is in all humbleness. But that old mounted duck serves another very important purpose in my life, and when I look at it I cannot help but move back across the years, reflecting on a winter afternoon that changed my life forever as a hunter.

After a year or so of hunting the swamp, Don Flynn and I figured out where the very core of the wood duck roost was. There was a power line right-of-way that cut through one corner of the swamp, and it had grown up with buttonbush. This thick growth gave the ducks security from marauding owls during the night. There was virtually no way for an owl to make a successful attack through all the tangle. And as for other predators (including duck hunters), there was no way to approach without making an awful lot of racket. So, once a duck was in that brush, it was safe.

During most of the duck season we were very careful not to get too close to that roost. We didn't want to frighten "our" ducks and thereby risk running them off from the swamp for the rest of the season. But in the final days of the season, we geared up for a grand finale hunt that featured that roost. Since legal shooting time stops at sunset, even for our grand finale hunt we'd be done shooting before most of the wood ducks came in.

I was a senior in high school at the time and I wanted a drake wood duck mounted. In fact, all of us boys in the old Explorer Boy Scout troop wanted one. We'd killed *a lot* of ducks (maybe eight to ten apiece) during the season but typically they had a shot-up wing or beak or foot and so were not appropriate for mounting. We had to do something special to get the trophies we wanted. So, we decided to hunt the roost with light bird loads and open-choked shotgun barrels. The small shot wouldn't mess up the birds and the spread-out shot charge would limit the number of pellet strikes. If we were careful and picked our shots, we'd be able to get the ducks we wanted.

Don Flynn and I shared our secret of the swamp roost with three other close friends, Sam Gates, Aniel House, and Mike Kelly. The hunt was planned for late afternoon on the second Saturday of January, just as the season was coming to a close. We assembled at Mike's house and piled into his old Jeep with our shotguns and hip boots. We didn't need decoys. The ducks would come regardless.

We parked the Jeep on the other end of the swamp road from where our normal parking place was in order to be closer to the roost and minimize the amount of time that five boys with shotguns would be seen walking along the road. The plan worked and we were able to get into the swamp without being seen. Then we slogged and sloshed our way along the edge of the brushy right-of-way until we were a couple of hundred yards away from the road. Don Flynn wanted to hunt alone farther along the right-of-way. Aniel and Mike wanted to hunt together toward the middle of the roost. Sam and I would hunt on the end of the roost closest to the road.

We synchronized our watches and warned each other not to shoot past quitting time. Then we split up and took our positions.

The brush was so thick that I couldn't see more than about twenty feet into it. This was going to be tricky. I heard Sam sloshing back in the brush, but I couldn't see him. I whistled to him and he whistled back.

"Sam," I cautioned, "we've got to be real careful. We're pretty close together and we can't see each other."

"Yeah, I know," he replied. "Man, this stuff is thick. At least we know that there won't be any low shots. The only way I can see to shoot is almost straight up."

"Well, anyway, I think we better stay put in one spot so we'll know where we are, O.K.?"

"Right on."

About 4:30 we heard a shot from down along the brush line, then a couple of shots closer to us. The ducks were on their way.

A wood duck wheeled past me and did a nose dive into the brush and disappeared. Then another one came in and did the same thing. I didn't have a chance to shoot at either one of them. One came in high overhead and Sam shot. The duck folded and I heard it hit the water. Then another one came by and I saw that it was a drake.

I waited until the duck was just in the right spot and shot. Down he came, but he wasn't dead. The light loads and the open-choked barrel had done their job in bringing the duck down, but now I had a cripple on the water. And he was swimming away from me.

I took careful aim, held over the duck just a little so as not to put the full charge of shot on him, and fired.

The duck flipped over dead, and simultaneously there was a scream and a yell back in the bushes! I'd shot Sam! The shot had ricocheted off the surface of the water, and unknown to me, Sam had moved from his shooting spot to get the duck he'd shot. He had been directly in my line of fire when I'd shot.

"Jesus Christ!" I shouted.

"Buddy! You shot me!" Sam hollered.

"Are you hurt bad?!"

"No, I had my back to you, but some of the shot are in the back of my neck."

"Sam! I'm on my way. Stay put. Hey, Aniel, I just shot Sam!"

"Hey, y'all," Sam shouted. "I'm not hurt bad, keep on hunting. I'm going on over to pick up my duck. Jackson, did you get yours?"

"Sam, get out of those bushes and meet me in the woods. Damn, I'm sorry. I had no idea that you were over there. Damn!"

I could hear Sam sloshing around. I went over, picked up my duck, and then walked over to meet Sam. He had a big grin on his face and a beautiful drake wood duck in his hands. He didn't look like a man that had just been shot, so I figured he was in shock.

When he got over to me he said, "Jackson, it just stung me a little. I'm not hurt."

"Let me take a look," I answered.

The back of his neck was all puffed up with little red bumps, and inside about a half a dozen of those bumps were little black dots, shot from my gun.

"We've got to get those shot out of you, Sam," I said.

"Hey, buddy, this hunt's about over anyway. Let's finish it and then you can pick out the shot once we get back to the house."

I didn't feel like hunting, but Sam was determined. He shouted back to the rest of the group that he was O.K., and their response was a new volley of shots as another wave of ducks came in. My gun, however, was unloaded, and I was feeling very, very sick to my stomach. I'd just shot my friend, and there was no way to go back in time and erase it.

By the time we got back to the Jeep, everybody was laughing about it except me. I felt about as low as a snake's belly. Sure, Sam had moved, but that was no excuse. It was me and my gun that had shot him. That drake duck could have gotten away. I knew that shot would ricochet off water. I also knew that there would be more ducks coming. Losing a duck is better than losing a friend.

Sam kept his promise when we got to his house. He wouldn't let anybody but me take the shot out of his neck. Each one hurt so bad. Sam laughed as I probed the wounds with tweezers, his head on a pillow on the kitchen table, his hands clutching the edge of the table. I cried.

Now, after three decades, when I look at my duck on the wall over my bed, I can still hear those number eight shot hit the bottom of the plastic vial . . . one at a time. And they hurt as much now as they did then.

I'll never take that duck down.

. . .

My family moved from Arkansas to Alabama when I was in my first year at the University of Arkansas. I think my parents thought I'd jump at the chance to switch from a zoology major at the University of Arkansas to a wildlife management or fisheries management major at Auburn University. But I'd already fallen in love with the Ozarks, and besides, Arkansas was my home. I wasn't about to leave my buddies and hunting and fishing spots. I'd *visit* family in Alabama, but then I'd *come home* to Arkansas. I think it broke my mother's heart, but then I think all mothers' hearts are broken when their oldest child grows up enough to leave the nest. Young men have to eventually blaze their own trail.

It was the last week of December the year after my folks had moved to Alabama, and I was blazing that trail back to the Ozarks and the university after two weeks of Christmas break. I was a college sophomore then and on an academic roll. All through the previous autumn, I had not hunted. All I'd done was study and try to figure out what was going on with a very pretty, half Cherokee girl who had decided I belonged to her (and I'd decided over the holidays that I did not!). As a sort of bonus Christmas gift for me while in Alabama, my dad had arranged for me to go on a quail hunt with one of the men who attended the church where my dad served as minister. So in the trunk of my car I had my hunting stuff.

I was scheduled to spend the night with my dear friends, Al and Francis Bing, in North Little Rock. Al and Francis were an elderly couple who had never had children. They had semi-adopted me as a boy, and Al had been my mentor in hunting, fishing, gun safety, and other essentials. As I pulled into North Little Rock that December afternoon it dawned on me that I was really too early to go to the Bings' house but not too early for an afternoon duck hunt out in the swamp. So instead of taking the exit off the interstate highway leading to the residential community called Lakewood, I kept on going straight to the next exit that led to the swamp road.

When I got to the road I went to my old parking place, and sure enough, there was still a little gravel there. I opened my car's trunk, pulled out my hunting coat, hip boots, and shotgun, got dressed, and headed down the road to "the trail." It was one of those golden winter afternoons. The temperature was in the low forties. The sky was a deep clear blue. There wasn't a breath of wind. The reflections in the water were perfect.

As I waded out into the swamp, I figured I'd just ease on over to the wood duck roost and bust a couple of ducks. It was nearly the end of the season anyway, and besides, I didn't figure anybody ever hunted the place. I didn't have any decoys and didn't think I'd need them. This was a wood duck hunt. I also did not have a duck call. And the only shot I had were some light load #8 shot that I'd used for the Alabama quail hunt. My "duck barrel" was still in my dormitory room up in Fayetteville. All I had was the short, open-choked "bird barrel." I figured I had the right outfit for wood ducks coming into their roost.

I was still haunted by memories of shooting Sam Gates during our wood duck hunt in that brushy roost area, and so decided I'd just hunt at the edge of it. I thought to myself, "What if some new high school kid has found this duck hunting place and has slipped in there for a late season roost shoot and I don't know it." I needed enough open space around me to be able to see where I was shooting. And that decision to stay in an open space turned out to be the catalyst for one of my most memorable hunts in the swamp.

The afternoon deepened and assumed the wonderful mysterious character that only a swamp in the Deep South can have as a day draws to an end. The sun cast its glow through the trees. Fox squirrels scratched and barked and jumped around in the branches and vines of the old tupelo gum trees that surrounded me. In the distance I could see the beginnings of the evening wood duck flight and got myself ready. Then I looked up for some reason, and saw, very high and lined out like they were headed for the Gulf of Mexico, a big flight of mallards. Aside from the three mallards I'd seen the day I'd hunted alone and killed that big drake, these were the only mallards I'd ever seen in the swamp and the only big flock. There were perhaps thirty or forty ducks and there I stood, with no decoys, no call, no heavy shot loads, and no tight-choked gun barrel. There was nothing to lose.

I quacked at them . . . with my mouth. I quacked with the best highball call I could produce, and lo and behold, they turned. I quacked again and they quacked back. Then I started the feeding call chuckle, again with my mouth. The mallards dropped to treetop level and began circling. I couldn't believe it! They circled twice and then came right over me, necks stretched, looking for those invisible ducks on the water. I knew that they wouldn't circle again; there were no decoys to get their attention and they were too close now to believe that funny quacking I was making with my mouth.

I raised my gun, held on the duck closest to me, and fired. It was a hen, and down she came through the branches—straight for me! I tried to dodge but she hit me in the head and knocked off my hunting hat. I recovered myself quickly and pulled on a drake. He folded at my shot, stone cold dead, and plopped with a huge splash into the water about fifteen feet from me.

"Lord have mercy!" I thought. "Is this for real?"

It was.

And it was also my last hunt in the swamp.

Since that last hunt I did eventually make it to Auburn University and from there became a fisheries professor at Mississippi State University. It's been my good fortune to have hunted ducks in lots of places across the country, including some of the best places in Alaska. I now have too many shotguns, but the only one I can hit with is an old smooth-barrel 12 gauge. I don't have a swamp anymore but I do have a pond out on my farm that has an open area for mallards and a brushy island out in the middle of it where a hunter with a partner or two can hide in among the willows. I hunt it regularly during the duck season, and it is a pretty steady place. Located between a nearby national wildlife refuge and a big wetland area north of me, it sits on a sort of flyway for ducks. Just about every morning that I hunt I can expect a flock or two of ducks to drift in, and I usually get a shot or two before it's time to pack up and get on to work at the university.

But there's another pond tucked back in the woods on the place, the "wild pond," that is choked with buttonbush that the wood ducks use as a roost during the wintertime. When I'm down in the woods by our wild pond, the same magic that once oozed from the old swamp over in Arkansas is also there . . . especially when one of my young'n's says, "Shsss, Papa, look, they're coming in, get ready."

Thirty years after my last hunt in the swamp, while in North Little Rock visiting friends, I decided to drive out to see if the old swamp was still there. It was. Businesses and residential areas surrounded it, but for whatever reason that tiny tupelo gum swamp had survived. I could still recognize the trail to the duck hole, and the buttonbush roost was as thick as ever. I closed my eyes, took a deep breath of swamp air, and listened carefully. Drifting through those flooded woods, ever so faintly, came the echo of boys' voices. The strange warmth I'd felt when I'd let the old fox squirrel go swelled up inside of me.

Wild Pond Woodies

Back in the woods on my little farm in Mississippi, down below my big pond, there's a small, brush-choked pond that typically dries up during the summer. It was built a long time ago, probably by someone using mules and some sort of scraper. Trees grow all around it, including on its levee. Even when it is full, nowhere is it more than four feet deep. It has probably been there for over fifty years.

It's a haven for salamanders and frogs, particularly during late winter and early spring, because there are no fish in it to eat them or their eggs and tadpoles. If for no other reason than this, it is a treasure. The summer drying also encourages the buttonbush that grows in a thick stand around its periphery. After the bottom hardens in midsummer I can get in the middle of it all with a chainsaw to keep an opening cleared. I leave the stand thick around the edges, however, so that wood ducks that want to roost there can have some protection from owls.

Three wood duck nest boxes are positioned nearby on posts. The posts have predator guards on them to keep raccoons from eating duck eggs in the boxes. I clean the boxes once each year, removing old cedar shavings and egg fragments. Usually by April or May, I have wood duck hens in all of the boxes. On the bigger pond I have two nest boxes. However, there the wood ducks have to compete with hooded mergansers for the nest boxes. Back on the wild pond, wood ducks prevail.

I'm a duck hunter. I love to chase blue-winged teal as they buzz the mud flats in September. Flooded woods casts a spell on me as mallards float into my decoys. My heart swells with visions of divers, bluebills, and ringnecks, as they come roaring in full of muscle and determination low over open water. The sparkle of midwinter mornings on rice fields touches my soul as pintails, widgeon, and gadwalls circle. Memories of days spent on Alaska's Stikine River flats, shooting pintails and sandhill cranes, are precious to me. But for some reason wood ducks have through the years become my favorite.

Wood ducks are beautiful birds. They are also just about the best duck to eat that there is, second only to teal and considerably better than mallard. But my love for wood ducks transcends these attributes. There's something about how and where they live that fascinates me. They certainly can migrate and can move in big groups. The very first duck I ever shot as a boy in Arkansas was a wood duck hen from a creek named Bayou Meto. She had a band on her leg. I sent in the number to the U.S. Fish and Wildlife Service and they reported that she had been banded two weeks earlier on an island up on Lake Michigan! But they're also the "local" duck, the "summer" duck, given to living in pairs or small groups in tiny backwater places, along quiet corners of slow, meandering streams, sloughs, and hidden spots like my wild pond down in the Deep South. They also respond well to nurturing. Give them a place to nest and a place to live and they'll be there.

They are puddle ducks, like mallards, teal, gadwalls, and pintails, but, unlike other puddle ducks, they don't cup their wings and float into decoys when landing. Wood ducks don't know how to do anything slowly when they are in the air. They fly hard and fast. They land hard and fast. They take off hard and fast. In the open, they fly in straight lines, but, down in the woods, they are masters of twisting and turning on the wing. In that sense, and in their world, they are just about the toughest duck to hit with a shotgun that there is. They make this doubly tough by their propensity to land right on top of you. A duck at a range of five or ten feet is not a duck you can shoot at. And by the time that duck has taken off and is at a decent distance for shooting, it's usually cranked up and twisting through the trees so that hitting it is more a matter of luck than skill. And when they're coming in or taking off, they get right on top of you and let out a squeal designed to unnerve you. It almost always works.

So, I've more or less christened them as my favorite. Any duck that will live with me all year long, glide as jewels on the surface of my ponds, fill the dawns and dusks with whistling wings and squeals, let me help it raise its families, let me shoot *at* it two or three times a week during the winter hunting season, and occasionally graces my table at dinnertime just has too much going for it to be rated anything other than the top slot in the duck hierarchy.

The year 2002 was especially good for wood ducks. We'd suffered together through five years of drought, but it finally broke, and, with the coming of the rains, wood ducks came on strong. There were little wood ducks everywhere. The nest boxes and hollow trees became duck factories. The low spots in the woods were wet most of the summer. My wild pond filled and stayed that way. My woods were filled with the sound of wood duck wings and squeals.

Duck season opened in November, and the first week I made a point of hunting my big pond instead of going to the wild pond. I wanted to save that place for a special hunt during the Thanksgiving holidays. My two sons would be out of school and my parents would be driving down from Florence, Alabama, to share Thanksgiving with us. I planned to take my boys and my father on a wild pond wood duck hunt.

On the big pond that week, an occasional duck would swing by, and I'd take a crack at it. I got a few, but the major flight in the morning centered on my wild pond. I'd stand there watching from a distance as they poured into that little place, in pairs, small groups, and singles until I began to wonder if there was room for another duck. But it was all over by the time the sun rose.

Wood ducks are early morning birds. Other ducks, the big ducks like mallards and gadwalls, come later in the morning. Wood ducks work their magic at the crack of dawn. I think they do this also to make it harder for hunters to shoot. Not only are they masters at using trees to their advantage; they also know the power of shadows that linger in their hidden little spots. They'll get up, and, instead of flying up and away, they'll hug the water so that they're virtually invisible in the early minutes of legal shooting time, and by the time they get up into the light, they're already on their way and gone (they don't do this later in the morning). They also play with the shadows in much the same way as they come in for a landing. If you are not set up just right, you can have ducks all over you, swimming around your feet, then beating you to death with their wings, or at least knocking off your hunting hat, and by the end of the pre-sunrise flight you probably will have no duck and quite likely will not even have had the opportunity for a shot. Then it is all over and you might as well go home.

Thanksgiving Day came, and with it there was an afternoon walk around the farm with boys, Grandma and Grandpa, and the dogs. One boy, two dogs, and Grandma went down to the wild pond to check it out. Grandpa and I stayed up on the levee of the big pond to watch the show. Suddenly, wood ducks filled the air all around us. There must have been more than sixty of them down on that wild pond. They just kept on getting up and whirling around the big pond and the adjacent pasture. I'd had no idea that there were that many. I'd figured on around twenty birds; that would be enough for our hunt. But never had I expected as many as there were. Since it was pretty late in the afternoon, they all just went on ahead to wherever it is that they roost. I knew they'd be back the following morning.

A wood duck hunt on my wild pond is probably the easiest duck hunt logistically in existence. There's no need for decoys. The ducks come to the pond regardless. There's no need for a blind or a boat or even high boots because you can stand on dry ground, beside a tree on the pond levee. The dogs go out into the water to get the birds, if there are any birds to get. If birds fall beyond the pond, it's in fairly open woods or pasture beside the big pond. If there was ever a "gentleman's" hunt, it is a wood duck hunt on my wild pond. But you still have to hit the things. That's where the rub comes in.

Grandpa wouldn't be shooting on this hunt. He just wanted to watch the pageantry of it all. I positioned one boy on one end of the pond and another toward the middle. After reminders regarding shooting safety to both of them, including no low shots, I shuffled down to the far end of the pond with the dogs. I tied them up so that they wouldn't start running around looking for downed ducks when other ducks were trying to come in. There would be plenty of time to pick up ducks after the morning flight was over.

Then the magic began. The ducks came right on schedule, zipping, darting, and crashing into that little pond. They came in little groups of five or six ducks, pairs, singles, twisting, squealing, filling the air with the sound of their wings. I heard shots from the other end of the pond and then suddenly it was my turn. A hen came whipping by me; I swung, shot, and saw her tumble down. Another small group roared in and landed on top of me. I was wearing my waders and standing out in about three feet of water. Ducks were swimming all around my boots. When they got up, I had one clean shot, took it and missed. One of my sons called to me to help him get a duck he had down on the water. I released the dogs and went over to him. Just then, another small flock came in and there was a shot and another duck on the water. Ducks just kept piling in on top of us. It was an absolutely incredible spectacle.

It didn't matter that I was out in the water with the dogs trying to retrieve a duck. They just kept on coming. Finally, I was in position again to shoot and made a very fast but very clean shot on a duck that had come in, looked over the situation, and decided it wasn't the right place to be that morning. I had my two ducks. David had his two ducks. Robert (my artist) was just capturing it all in his mind, soaking up the beauty of the morning and all that went into it. He's a very special hunting companion in that regard. Grandpa was beside himself, knowing that he'd just witnessed something very, very special.

Then it was all over. The sun rose. We had our ducks. Shotguns were unloaded and boys and dogs released from the discipline of the hunt. Grandpa and

I followed them, through the woods and up the levee to the big pond, then started across the pasture to the truck. I heard a whistle of wings and a squeal. Turning, I saw a dozen ducks drop from the treeline into the wild pond. I could hear the hen wood ducks calling to their drakes and splashing around. I handed the duck strap with our four ducks to David, slung my shotgun across my shoulders, and, with a smile, knew where I'd be the following morning. There could be one more hunt and then I'd have to let the wild pond and the ducks rest for a few days.

The next morning I hunted alone. The boys had other plans for their Saturday and my parents had returned home. The dogs were with me, tied to their spots along the levee of the wild pond. I carefully slipped down into the water, positioning myself against a tree in a way where I could see almost the entire pond and have the most open area for shooting.

Right on schedule, three ducks came roaring in. I swung on a drake, shot, and down he came. The others landed but quickly swam to the far end of the pond. Then a hen came in and landed before I could get my gun up. I watched her swim around for a while in the shadows across the pond from me, then kicked at the water to get her up. She hesitated for a moment, then got up, giving me a perfect right to left shot. I let her get out over the buttonbush just a little before shooting so that I'd have a good but not too dense shot pattern. Everything connected perfectly, and I had my second duck on the water.

Climbing up out of the pond, I released the dogs and each dog got to retrieve one of the ducks. Then, as quickly as we could, we left, and as had happened the day before, ducks came to the pond after we'd gotten to the top of the big pond's levee. These new ducks were not spooked, and we left them in peace. As we walked across the pasture wild geese started flying overhead. They were snows and blues, common in the Delta but not normally found in this part of Mississippi where Canada geese reign. I just stood and watched them, listening to their high-pitched calls until they passed out of sight and earshot.

I thought then to myself how very special it was to have my own place . . . a little piece of heaven here in Mississippi where I can come to ramble around in the wild, where I can slip into a woodland pond early on a winter's morning, shoot a couple of ducks, watch geese fly overhead, perhaps see a deer, spot a raccoon track in the mud alongside my creek, listen to the predawn chorus of coyotes, and greet the sunrise with a very special sort of prayer, with ducks, shotguns, and dogs as my sacraments. There are some things that finally fall into place after a man has logged fifty years or so.

For the following two weeks I had regular encounters with the pond and the ducks. I am not totally addicted to it all but almost. All the while, however, plans were being made for our family to fly to Panama for Christmas with my wife's family. But we wouldn't all go together. Pending war with Arabs and the threats of terrorism from them on the home front made it unwise for us to fly together as a family before Christmas. The threats wouldn't be so bad after Christmas. So my wife and two youngest children would go down to Panama first. I'd follow a few days later with my older son. He had final exams to deal with during that week which only added to reasons for us to come down later.

The extra days in Mississippi were gifts for me. I could hunt early in the mornings and get home in time to take Robert on to school. Most of the hunts were successful, with a duck or two on the strap as I walked back to the truck. On the Friday that we were to drive to New Orleans to catch our flight, I shot two wood ducks from the wild pond, one for each dog to retrieve, before taking the dogs to the boarding kennel. It was good for my soul as well as for the dogs.

I'm writing all of this on New Year's Eve down in Panama. We've had a fine visit with family and with the world in general here. My wife has reconnected with her culture. I've enjoyed the relaxed pace and seeing a few friends from my old graduate school days. We've traveled around some, gone jungle tromping, beach swimming, and fishing for peacock bass in the Chagres River where it flows into the Panama Canal. A few days ago, we took a trip out into the countryside to a big volcanic crater a couple of hours' drive west of Panama City. The area we visited is high, cool, clean, and pretty much a vacation spot with nice homes and gardens. One of the places where we stopped was a botanical garden. There was a pond in the garden, and there, gliding around on the water, preening on the pond bank were, of all things—wood ducks! The encounter was good for my soul because duck season is in full swing back in Mississippi and, although it is good to be here with family, my dreams at night tend to be full of wings and squeals and visions of grey dawns reflecting on pond water.

I took a deep breath and smiled. By the time we get back home this coming Friday evening, my wild pond and the wood ducks on it will have had two full weeks to rest. New ducks probably will have filtered into the area and teamed up with the local ducks that use my pond. Come Saturday morning, I'll be standing beside my tree at the edge of the pond. I'll be loading my shotgun with number four steel shot as the light just begins to filter in through the tree branches. I'll strain to see the time on my watch, getting set for legal shooting time. Then the countdown as seconds tick off . . . a sudden rush of wings, probably a squeal, quickly followed by twisting ducks coming in through the treetops hard and fast . . . a split second of opportunity and, if all the components fit together, there will be a shot, a splash, and a whining dog ready and about to get wet.

Postscript: Four wood ducks came in. One got past me before I could shoot. I missed one, then swung and got a double.

Connections of a Feathery Sort

"Are those guns broken down, boys?"

The bus driver in Little Rock wrinkled his brow at us and frowned to let us know that he meant business, but then he broke into a smile.

"Yes, sir," we replied as we took our seats on a hot August afternoon and stowed our shotguns, zipped up tightly inside their soft cases, on the racks above our heads.

"Where're y'all headed?" he asked.

"Up to my grandmother's place in Mississippi County for a dove hunt," I replied. "The season opens tomorrow."

Back in the late 1960s, boys with shotguns in bus stations and on buses were looked at as boys with shotguns in bus stations and on buses—nothing else. The idea of there being anything amiss simply didn't enter into people's minds. There was a war going on in Southeast Asia at the time. Most of us boys in high school figured that we were probably headed that way, and that pretty much took the zip out of any deviant tendencies we might have had on the domestic side of the creek. And anyway, the sort of young fellows that caused trouble, "hoods," we called them, used switchblade knives, not guns, and they lived in cities like New York, Chicago, and Los Angeles, not in places like Memphis, Little Rock, Dallas, and Atlanta. You were safe as long as you stayed at home in the South. There weren't "hoods" in our cities. Fifteen-year-old boys with shotguns in the South were going hunting, and hunting was considered a proper thing for boys to do.

We took our seats and settled down for the two-hour ride up to West Memphis. My running buddy, Don Flynn, and I felt pretty puffed up. Here we were, darn near grown (we thought), traveling alone across America with guns, our suitcases jam-packed full of shotgun shells, headed out "adventuring" more than 125 miles away for a rendezvous with my uncle Bob. Uncle Bob would meet us at the West Memphis bus station and haul us in his pickup truck out to my grandmother's farm in a little community called Whitton. School didn't start for another week. Heaven couldn't possibly be any sweeter.

The tupelo and cypress breaks flashed by outside the bus windows. We crossed the big mysterious rivers, the White, the Cache, and the Saint Francis, and wondered what lay beyond the bends. Rice fields swayed like green carpets, and cotton and soybean fields stretched nearly from horizon to horizon, broken only by distant stands of timber. The sky was so bright that you had to squint to look at it and at the clouds that billowed up as the day got hotter. We could see doves perched on the power lines and occasionally see them flitting across open spaces as the bus sped on.

My uncle was waiting for us when the bus pulled into the station. We put our guns and suitcases in the back of his old truck and rumbled out of town. He told us that my grandmother, Nettie, had lunch ready for us and that we didn't want to dillydally around . . . wouldn't be nice. Once out of town we were deep in the world of tractors, crop dusters, gins, dusty roads, and weedy ditch banks. Around the houses and tiny country churches were ancient trees, gnarled old walnuts or huge stately oaks. Next to the houses were rose and snowball bushes. Some folks still had chickens in their yards, and almost everyone had a garden of some sort. There were pecan groves and twisted old pear trees. The doors and "air pipes" of storm cellars stuck up out of yards behind the houses. Where the yards ended, the cotton and soybean fields began.

As we pulled into my grandmother's driveway, past the big walnut tree out by the gravel road, she met us at the door of her screened-in front porch. There was a hush on the dusty land, broken only by the distant sound of a tractor somewhere and the occasional crunch of gravel as someone drove by. "Y'all get out and come on in," she said with a grin. "Lunch is ready. Bet you boys are starved."

Just about the only time I ever left my cherished shotgun unattended was when I was at school or church or bolting out of a car to go give my grandmother a hug. As I gave her that hug I realized for the first time just how small she was. Perhaps it was because on that day, my first long-distance, all-by-myself hunt, I actually felt pretty big (also for the first time in my life). I'd always been sort of a runt, and usually was the smallest boy in class. But for the past year I'd been growing about an inch a month and putting on muscle from the marine corps exercise routine I'd been maintaining. (Much to the recruiter's pleasure, I'd been sneaking over to Little Rock about once a month and talking to him about enlisting and going off to war to help my friends win that thing. The recruiter had given me the exercise schedule for boot camp and I was getting ready for both the marines and the war. I couldn't envision a future beyond that.)

After the hugs, I went back to the truck where Flynn (we always called each other by our last names) was unloading. I got my stuff out of the truck and Uncle Bob said he'd come back for us in a while so that we could scout. Then he was off to have lunch at his house, which sat up under some pecan trees about half a mile up the road behind my grandmother's house.

We stowed our gear in the back bedroom of my grandmother's house, where my uncle Bob used to live before he got married. It was always cool back there in that room in the summertime (cold in the winter) and sort of musty smelling. I liked that smell. It smelled old but clean, like a home is supposed to smell. The hardwood floor creaked as we walked on it. Light filtered through the curtains. The screened windows let in the soft sounds of late summer in the Delta . . . chickens clucking, bees humming, tractors droning. The sheets and towels and quilts were all fresh and ready for us. We washed up in the bathroom, returned to the dining room, and dived into the grub that Grandmother had spread all across the dining room table beside the bay window. We only paused long enough to say a short grace (but with eyeballs already glued on the food).

What a lunch it was. There was creamed corn, fried chicken, fried okra, sliced tomatoes as big as a saucer, cole slaw, yellow squash, buttered hot rolls that tended to float off the plate and right into your mouth, and about a gallon of cold milk for each of us. Fifteen-year-old boys can really put away the grub, and we didn't let the reputation slip.

Then came dessert. There was apple pie so tart and sweet that just to think of it makes tears begin to roll. And on top of it all was homemade peach ice cream. By the time we were done we were as full as ticks. Lord, what a spread my grandmother could put together.

Then the phone rang, a long and a short (my grandmother was on a party line). It was my uncle Bob. He and his hired hand, Joel D. Lindley, were coming by in a couple of minutes to pick us up and show us around the country so that we could spot places to hunt the next day. My grandmother told us to get out of the house, that she would tend to the dishes. She said that she fully expected us to bring in a sack of doves the following day so that she could cook up a good smothered dove dinner.

And how could we get the doves if we didn't scout the land to find out where they were?

My grandmother knew how to talk to hunters—especially when they were two gangly Arkansas boys and one was her grandson. Flynn fell in love with her immediately. She was a dandy.

Uncle Bob and Joel D. rumbled into the front yard and pulled to a stop in front of Grandmother's concrete front steps. Flynn and I jumped into the bed of the truck and off we went.

What an absolute riot it is to go hauling around the countryside of eastern Arkansas in the back of your uncle's pickup. The hot, dry wind tugged at our hair. The dusty landscape shimmered in the late summer sun. There was the smell of defoliant in the air as folks got ready for picking cotton. In the shops the cotton pickers and combines were surrounded by men making repairs and adjustments. Out in the fields the bolls hung heavy and ripe from late plantings or were like snow from the fortunate few that had been able to get the crops planted early. The soybeans were just beginning to have a yellow tint to them. The ditches were mostly just trickles of water. The Tyronza River was low and about as clear as a Delta stream can get. I breathed deep, connecting again with the land and the culture.

This was a place where I belonged and where, as a Jackson, I could go just about anywhere and do just about anything. Doors always opened. Permission was always granted. Nobody ever said no.

Our family had been in the Delta a long time. Our roots stretched way back, even to before the War Between the States. When I was little, my grandmother had told me stories about the big woods and the covered wagons and the panthers, and about my grandfather, whom I'd never seen (he died when my father was thirteen). He'd been a wheeler and a dealer, a big land owner, bass fisherman, goose and quail hunter, and sort of a director of the old Dyce Colony, which was one of the first socialist experiments in the country.

I'd sit there on the big swing beside her, looking out across the field in front of her house, to Dead Timber Lake, with all of its mysteries as the day turned dusky and night critters started to drift out of the shadows, rustling the bushes and chirping and scratching, and I'd drift off to those long-gone years, and those long-gone woods. The land and its history cast a spell on me that lingers yet deep in my soul.

I didn't abuse my privileges or risk my family name. I just wasn't brought up to cross the line. To bring dishonor to the family was unthinkable. I guess that was why those doors always opened. I could end up around lunchtime at Miss Tin Wright's house down back of the big trees across the road by the lake, or up at Bob Gammel's or Jess Forester's and there would be an invitation to come in for a bite. Or I could be sweating and covered with dust and be over by Mr. Denton's gin and Mr. Denton would say, "Boys, you look like you could handle a NuGrape or a Palmac." Then he'd dig around in the big drink cooler and haul out the bottles all covered with icy dew and you couldn't drink it fast enough. And when my uncle Bob's big Tennessee walking horse would get cantankerous and buck me off and I'd wander over to some sharecropper's house to get some water to wash off the scrapes, there'd be iced tea and maybe some banana nut bread. I was John's boy and the whole world was mine if I wanted it.

That afternoon driving around the county, "home turf" we called it, we saw the doves that we were about to declare war on. They were on the telephone wires that stretched along the dusty roads. They were perched in the highest bare branches of honey locust trees. They were around the wet places, the ditch banks, twisting and darting above the Johnson grass that grew along the river, and fluttering in behind people's barns to the puddles where water seeped from leaky pipes and hydrants. There also were a few small flocks, three to perhaps half a dozen birds at a time, over on the "upper place" where Joel D. had accidently spilled a couple of hundred pounds of wheat across three acres of disked land the week before, about the time I'd telephoned my grandmother to confirm that Don Flynn and I were coming for a hunt.

We really didn't see any great concentrations of doves, but we saw enough birds to know that there'd be shooting. It wasn't like it is nowadays. Nobody back then really got set up for doves in that part of the country, and nobody really hunted doves in a big way. Nowadays the big commercial hunting outfits all across the South have hundreds of acres of sunflowers planted just for doves and charge folks fifty dollars for a morning or afternoon shoot. Occasionally back then somebody might organize some shoot for his friends over a disked and baited field, but that was just about it. There wasn't much corn planted in those days in the Delta, not like now anyway, and besides, that time of the year folks over in Mississippi County were pretty busy getting ready for cotton picking and combining beans. So, it was just us—ole Flynn and me, two high school boys with our guns, with everybody else just sort of cheering us on.

As we pulled back into the yard in front of my grandmother's house that evening the sun hung like an orange ball over Dead Timber Lake. An early flock of teal skimmed over the water on the far side of the lake and settled in for the night. As the sun melted into the timber way off on the other side of a big field across the lake and the first stars began to pop out, we pulled the screen door shut behind us and sat for a while in the big porch swing. An old owl drifted past the big walnut tree out front and then sort of slipped along the corner of the house. But the chickens had already gone to roost, and Mr. Owl drifted on across the field in frustration to better pickings somewhere else. Right after the owl left, a rabbit eased out of my grandmother's iris bed. We watched it until it got almost too dark to see it in the shadows. Nighthawks beat their irregular rhythms against the deepening sky, and locusts began to hum.

We were so pumped up with expectations, we could almost smell gunpowder, almost hear the whistle of wings, almost feel the dew seep through our tennis shoes. We couldn't sit still, so we left the porch and went back into our room to check and clean our guns and sort out our shotgun shells. We could hear my grandmother shuffling around in the kitchen, an occasional pot clanging, as she brought out big bowls of soup, slices of ham, a plate full of sliced tomatoes, and a pitcher of iced tea.

After supper Flynn and I walked back out to the front porch, took positions on the swing and just sat. I'm not sure people do much of that anymore. Just sitting on a porch in the night. We didn't say much. We just sat out there looking at the paint that was peeling off the screen frames and listening to the crickets. That was enough.

A quiet had settled over the house and the land. It was the awesome quiet of a Delta night, the sort of quiet that is thick and rich. It's a quiet that only the Deep South can produce, one that blends with the dark in a way that just sort of folds itself around you like a blanket. It makes a boy shiver even when the temperature is still in the nineties at 10:00 at night. It's like the shiver you get when you eat homemade ice cream too fast. A Delta night can be so sweet, so thick, so good, that you just have to suck it down even though you know that it will give you the chills for a while and maybe even set your head to swimming. A Delta night on the eve before the dove season wraps itself around boys and lets them know that there's something wonderful about just being a boy—not just any boy, but a boy about to go hunting on sacred land, land that folks, even some of his family a long time ago, fought to keep. They might have lost the war but they managed to keep the land, and that was really all that had ever mattered anyway.

As we sat out there on the porch, another sort of chill started to settle on us. It was the sort of chill that warriors sometimes get on the eve of a great battle, knowing that with the dawn there will be great testing. But we were hunters, not soldiers, and not just any sort of hunters. We were wing shooters, and as wing shooters we were well aware that doves can be the ultimate test.

Doves are the most unpredictable birds that ever flapped a wing. They come highballing in over you, all cranked up, and you start throwing shot up at them. They dip and dive and peel to the left and right, never in a straight line, coming or going or crossing hard and fast. And sometimes, when the internal calculations get themselves all sorted out and the eye and the hand and the head and the gun and the feet and the arms and shoulders get into some kind of instinctive mode, there is magic and old Mr. Dove becomes a big puff up in the air and down he comes. Every one is a miracle.

I sat out there on my grandmother's porch, in the dark, in the quiet, and shut my eyes, shivering, trying to envision tomorrow's sunrise. My mind drifted deeper and deeper into the night . . . deeper and deeper into time . . . on and on and on . . . and on . . . and . . .

The sun rose a generation later over a small disked field in the back corner of a Mississippi farm. The two boys were hunkered down in the weeds with the sun to their back. A big chocolate laborador retriever and a yellow shepherd sat beside them, licking dew from their wet fur. I went over the safety rules with the boys, making them repeat the rules after me, looking each one in the eye, and telling them that if they got care-less and shot each other, or the dogs, there would be no way that I could ever go home, and that I'd be destined to pick bananas in Guatemala for the rest of my life, a fugitive in exile.

"Watch the end of the gun barrel at all times. Don't cock the thing until the dove is on you and you're ready to shoot. No low shots and no shots when anybody is out in the field picking up a downed bird."

"Yes, sir, Papa," they said.

"O.K. then." I coached. "There's one gun between the two of you. I don't want either of you hogging it. Each of you gets thirty minutes and then you swap out. I'm going to sit down on the far end of the field across from your uncle Scott. Your cousin Alex will be with Uncle Scott. You've got plenty of shells here, a box apiece, and if you need more, there's more in the truck."

I picked up my old pump gun and wandered off to my hiding place. I looked back once, and it seemed incred-ible that I was looking at my sons. It ought to still be me and old Flynn scrooched down over there in those weeds. A flight of wood ducks passed over the edge of the woods and headed for the pond just beyond the trees. Then there was a whistle of wings and a shadow as an early dove skimmed low over the field in the predawn light.

My boys were on their own land. The pond was theirs, as were the woods and the fields and the hillside where the truck was parked. The dove field was small, only a couple of acres, but the birds were using it. The boys were where they belonged, in wet tennis shoes, a dusty disked field in front of them and birds were coming in . . . BAM . . . the dove kept on flying minus a couple of tail feathers. BAM and one darted over my brother Scott, who stood up, swung on the bird, and nailed the scoundrel. The race was on between my chocolate lab and the yellow mutt. The mutt won, snatched up the dove, and ran to me with feathers and a wide grin all over his face.

Somehow that yellow shepherd, pulled from a cardboard box at an elementary school PTA circus, had picked up on what hunting is all about and had turned into a first-class retriever. He grew up watching me work out in the backyard with my lab and just figured it all out by himself. He absolutely loved to retrieve, especially if there was a contest to it (beating out the old dog), or if there was water involved.

I'd hesitated at first to take him with me on hunting trips, but one day got brave, took him, and by jingo he performed like a champ. My older son, Robert, was so proud of his dog that day that he could have popped. And what a nose that mutt had. The old lab was mostly a sight retriever, but Robert's dog knew how to use his nose. So, it was only the right thing to do to bring both dogs on this Mississippi dove hunt . . . BAM . . . brother

Scott had another one fluttering down, then there was one over me and I got a shot . . . BAM . . .

"Hey, Papa! Good shot!"

The shooting started to get pretty steady, and I saw Robert stand up, swing on a dove that was ripping out over the field, and fire. The dove crumpled and hit the ground hard. Robert's grin was so big I could see it from where I stood, seventy-five yards away. His old yellow dog made a perfect retrieve and this time took the bird back to Robert. The scene was beautiful and etched forever in my mind.

The sun broke over the trees behind the boys, and it was tradeoff time with the 20 gauge that they were sharing. I whistled at Robert and pointed to my watch. He unloaded the gun and gave it to his younger brother, David. I heard David snap the gun closed.

Three doves flew right over him and he fired. All three kept on going, but just as they crossed in front of my brother, he stood up, fired twice, and knocked down two of them. One fell out in the field, but the other landed in thick brush behind him. I'd marked it down, so directed him to where I thought it was. Then . . . BAM . . . and this time it is the old lab making the retrieve. David had his bird, still flapping, in his hand. Brother Scott leaned over and came up with his bird, so I walked across the field to help David with his flapping dove. I took it from his hand, rapped its head across my gun barrel, and handed it back to him. He's a hunter, but I saw a little sadness in his eyes. He fought it back, but I told him that if he ever stops feeling a little sad when he shoots something then it was time for him to quit hunting. He loaded up again and hunkered back down in his hiding spot as I walked back to my place across the field.

Then, as if a dam had suddenly given way, the doves started pouring in, dipping and darting, whistling over the disked ground, flaring and ripping over us, the early morning sun glowing on their rosy breasts. I heard the regular crack of the little 410 shotgun that my nephew Alex was shooting. My sons, realizing the magic of the hour, began passing their shotgun back and fourth between them every five minutes or so, instead of the half hour intervals we'd agreed on earlier. The dogs were in constant motion running across the field picking up fallen birds.

"Papa! We're running out of shells!" David shouted.

"O.K.," I hollered back to him. "Leave the gun with Robert and hustle over to the truck with me for some more."

David scrambled out of the clump of Johnson grass he was hiding in and ran across the field to join me. As we walked around the little patch of woods to where the truck was parked, a pair of doves zipped overhead. I swung on the lead bird, fired, and the trailing bird dropped.

"Good shot, Papa!"

I kept my mouth shut.

Behind us was the constant "boom" of my brother's 12 gauge, the "bam" of Robert with the 20 gauge, and the crack of Alex's little 410. I reached behind the seat of my pickup truck and handed David a fresh box of shotgun shells for the 20 gauge. Then I reached into the ice chest, and turned around to give him two cans of cold lemonade to carry back with him. But by the time I'd turned around, he was already halfway back to his brother, his trail across the dry disked field marked by puffs of dust hanging briefly over the tracks made by a small boy's tennis shoes.

By 9:30 it had started to get hot, and we had some pretty thirsty boys on our hands. The rush of birds had begun to fade and there was only an occasional shot. I ambled over to where my brother and nephew were hunkered in tall weeds by an Osage orange tree. The grass was all tromped down, and there were empty shotgun shells strewn all over the ground. A neat pile of doves lay in the shadows of the tree. Alex told me that he'd shot two of the doves all by himself. He was in the process of describing exactly how it happened when a half a dozen doves came streaking right by in front of us. Alex pulled up his little shotgun, fired, and down came number three for the boy. I think he almost got to that bird before it hit the ground.

"Good shot, young man," I said as he came back to us with his bird in hand. "We're going to have to call you deadeye Alex from now on."

Sweat was beaded up on his forehead. The shade from the tree was fading fast. I unloaded my gun, looked out across the field, and saw my two boys on their way to us. It was time to go to the truck to get cold drinks. My brother told Alex to unload and gather up the birds. I could hear my boys talking to each other.

"Robert, you should have led that last dove more. Don't you remember that Papa said you've got to get way out in front of them?"

"I *did* shoot out in front of him, but just as I shot he dipped down to the ground, David. What about that one that tried to land in front of *you*. I guess that was a dead bird that flew away after you shot."

The boys came shuffling on across the dusty field, shotgun open and unloaded in David's arms, and a sack of doves dangling from Robert's hands. The dogs were at their sides, tongues lolled out and dripping. We met them at the edge of the woods and walked up the little hill to where the truck was parked in the shade.

I hauled out the ice chest and started passing the drinks around while the boys dumped their doves on the ground and started laying them out in rows across the tailgate of the truck. There were twenty-seven birds. I pulled another eight birds from my hunting vest pouch and laid them beside the others. The cicadas hummed and a yellow-billed cuckoo tonked back in the woods. We could hear the droning of a distant tractor. The smell of dust and freshly mowed pastures drifted on the breeze. The boys asked if they could go by themselves to the pond, and we turned them loose. Moments later we could hear them laughing and the dogs splashing as sticks were thrown into the water for the dogs to retrieve.

My brother and I just sat there, quietly, watching the wind ruffle the leaves of the oaks around us. A blue-jay called. The voices of boys came floating up through the woods.

"Hey, David! Look at all those doves that just landed in the field." "Papa! Can we come back this afternoon?!"

I took a deep breath, and closed my eyes. Time swirled. The rusty chain of the old wooden swing creaked on my grandmother's front porch. I took another long breath, feeling the rhythm of the swing like a clock's pendulum deep inside of me. The boy's shout was transformed into a whisper that echoed across the years. "Hey, Flynn, do you reckon we'll get to hunt together next year?"

Heritage

My great-grandfather, Joseph Jackson Rowe, was a young special forces scout in General Joe Wheeler's Confederate army. He fought all across north Alabama and into Tennessee. According to my family's oral history, he distinguished himself repeatedly in battle as an expert horseman and rifleman.

After the war he refused to surrender to the Yankees and just went home. Because he refused to surrender and in no small part because of his questionable activities as a special forces soldier, he became a hunted man during the early stages of Reconstruction. After dispatching an assassin sent to dispatch him, my great-grandfather found it in his best interest to change his name to Joel Jackson and to move from Georgia to Arkansas with my great-grandmother, Mary Ellen Hambrick, who was a Cherokee Indian.

They settled in the rich bottomlands along the White River in eastern Arkansas, where he had several scrapes with the law. Eventually he was pardoned for his war activities, was granted amnesty for his failure to surrender, was employed as a federal agent, and ultimately became postmaster for a small farming community near Newport, Arkansas. There's still a place in Newport called Jackson Point where my great-grandfather killed a man in a brawl. Apparently it was in self-defense. After the sheriff calmed the situation, he took my great-grandfather's army revolver away from him, just for the night.

My grandfather, Robert Andrew "Jack" Jackson, was one of Joel Jackson's fifteen children and a great sportsman. He was a respected and landed Delta farmer and also a sort of straw boss, taskmaster, and director for one of the nation's socialist experiments (Dyce Colony) in northeastern Arkansas. He hunted geese along the Mississippi River with live decoys, fished for bass in Delta streams back when those streams still ran clear, and he especially loved to hunt quail. Hunting and fishing were his passions.

I never knew my grandfather. He died while on an out-of-state business trip when my father, John, was thirteen years old, leaving my grandmother to raise their five children alone. Those were the Depression years, and times were tough on the Jackson family. But they had their land, and their spirit was strong. With help from the old Whitton community in Mississippi County where they lived, and especially from my grandfather's old hunting and fishing buddies, they made it, dignity and dreams intact.

It is said that I look like my grandfather, and that I act like him. When I was in high school, I inherited his old Remington shotgun. He'd had it custom made, with extra drop on a short stock so that it would come up fast when birds got up. For those unfamiliar with terms and value systems in the South, the word "birds" refers to only one species—quail. The shotgun was passed along to me by my uncle Bob, who, like my grandfather, was an avid sportsman.

Since I was the oldest grandson, it was only the right thing to do. Guns are like quilts and Bibles. They're history—in fact, more than history. They're heritage. Over the years I've reworked that old shotgun and, because the original stock was cracked, restocked it with the finest walnut. Only on very rare occasions do I shoot it. I'll pass it along someday.

That old gun is one of my treasures. But it was and continues to be, in reality, just a symbol of greater treasures given to me as a kid privileged to grow up in the South, things held not in the hands but in the heart. Perhaps they are more blessing than treasure. Fundamentally they centered on my having deep roots in the region. I knew as a boy that I belonged. I was linked to the South, its land and its history, by people who *were* history. Some were family, some were not. But regardless, there was kinship.

The heritage was passed along to me from a shared swing at sunset on ragged screened porches deep in lonesome woods, from fur sheds, smoky and dank and full of traps and stretcher boards, from storm cellars on raging spring nights, from gardens beside isolated share-cropper shacks down along tupelo gum breaks on July mornings with dew still on the plants, from the front yards of cabins beside oxbow lakes and cypress swamps that oozed mystery. The messages were accented by locusts whining, hens clucking, bees humming, mock-ingbirds calling, tractors droning, or the wind whisper-ing through ancient walnuts and oaks in front of the church after the sermon, benches worn slick by rough trousers down at the gin, or the rattle of hail on the door of the storm cellar.

We saw ourselves as stewards of a story . . . an eter-nal story. We spoke of settling the land and wresting a living from it. We spoke of struggles, mighty struggles, for independence, and of how in doing that wars seemed inevitable.

The Civil War had particular significance to us because it was still so fresh in the memories of many. It fact, it had much more significance to us than the First World War and seemed to give the Second World War a run for its money. However, we never really used the term "Civil War" because we were taught at an early age that there was nothing *civil* about it. In polite com-pany we referred to it as the War Between the States. But everyone really preferred to call it what it was, the War of Northern Aggression.

We had been invaded, ravaged, raped, and slaugh-tered by the Yankees. Our homes and cities were burned. Our crops were destroyed. Our livestock was killed. And, following the war, our women married rich Yankee army officers who realized that the only reason people would ever live north of the Mason-Dixon line was because they'd never lived south of it. (We'd been trying to tell them that for four long years!)

We were taught as children that the war really wasn't about slavery and that the history books had distorted the truth. It was about southern independence and states' rights. We had simply declared our independence. It was the North that invaded us, fired the first shots, and started the war. We acted in self-defense, fighting to force foreign invaders from our land.

The ancient ones who shared their wisdom and memories with my generation emphasized to us that in the years before the war, very few people actually owned slaves and that those who did were typically closely linked to them and their families. In fact, for most people, the "slaves" *were* family, and had been family for generations. They worked side by side with the whites on the farms. They helped establish churches. The children romped and tumbled around the countryside together, hunted and fished and swam and played together. They were like cousins and sometimes *were* cousins . . . all testimony of the inevitable blending of cultures and shared history.

Everyone back then knew that slavery, even in its most benign form, was wrong. Subsequently, slaves were being granted freedom throughout the region. The Emancipation Proclamation delivered by Abe Lincoln only reinforced what was already going on. Many freed slaves chose to continue working for their former masters and even assumed their family names. You just don't go around busting up or abandoning families and communities.

We were told that slavery didn't need a war to kill it. It was dying on its own. In fact, there were African American soldiers who fought for the Confederacy—entire companies of men (particularly from Louisiana) who knew, just as did the white soldiers, that we all deserved our independence and that what really was going on was an attempt by the Union to exploit our natural resources and to keep us under their thumb. We were taught that we had closer ties to Europe (especially France) than we had to the northern states. Slaves who "escaped" to the North, or freed slaves who moved there, soon found out that bigotry was more rampant up there than in most of the South. Homecomings were common after the war. They still are.

The currents of the old Confederacy ran deep in Arkansas when I was a young'n. We'd been a sovereign, independent nation. And we'd had a president, Jefferson Davis. We loved our country and our president. When I was growing up his name was always spoken with a tone of reverence. The old Confederate capitol, in Montgomery, Alabama, and Jefferson Davis's home, Beauvoir, on the Mississippi Gulf Coast, are still today almost sacred shrines to southerners. These places are open to the public and are much visited.

But there's another place, off limits to the general public, that oozes heritage and ghosts from the

Old South. Downstream from Vicksburg, over on the Louisiana side of the Mississippi River, is a little chunk of Mississippi cut off by the river from the rest of the state. It's called Davis Island. This island was President Jefferson Davis's plantation, Brierfield. To get there now other than by the river, you have to cross the river by the Vicksburg bridge, and drive all around Robin Hood's barn through Louisiana, down through back roads and along the main levee of the river, deeper and deeper into the woods, deeper and deeper into history, deeper and deeper into the spirit of the land and its people. It is perhaps *the* most hallowed ground of the South—more than Gettysburg (which is actually on Yankee soil), more than Shiloh, more than Antitum, more than Stone Mountain, even more than Vicksburg, our Gibralter. It was our president's land. And in the South, a man's land is the ultimate expression of his linkages with the currents of the universe. The connections are sacred. That's why we fought so hard during the war. Foreigners were on our land. Unless you're invited, you're not supposed to be on a man's land. This absolutely holds true for Davis Island. You absolutely can't set foot on this land without permission and escort. Don't even try.

After the war Brierfield passed into the hands of former slaves who maintained the plantation for many years. Theirs is a fabulous story of dedication and investment, of tragedy and triumph. They forged a community and lived with dreams that continue to echo across the land. But they, like the plantation's earlier owner, eventually succumbed to the economic and social realities of the evolving South and faded into the annals of history. And the land languished, until resurrected by men of vision who saw the land in new light—land that could reestablish the links between people and the earth. They bought it for hunting, and they developed plans to support their hunting clubs through forestry. But there was more to it than just the hunting and the economics. They knew it and so did everybody else. They were guardians of heritage.

In 1986, when I was thirty-five years old and living up in Alaska, I was asked to come home to the South. I'd been gone a long time, ripping and roaming around the world, tromping through Southeast Asian jungles, Australian deserts, and African plains, climbing among the world's tallest mountains in Nepal, and soaring through ethereal realms in seminary. But when the call came, I knew I had to heed it. Restless soul though I was, when a native son of the South is asked to come home, he does it.

So, I moved to Mississippi and joined the wildlife and fisheries faculty at Mississippi State University. My job was to keep the connection between people and rivers. The position required someone whose roots were deep in the land and the culture. The rivers had to run deep in his soul. The beat of the South had to be in synchrony with his heart. He had to be able to hear the whispers coming from the land. He had to speak the languages of both the old and the new South (and there are many). He had to believe in ghosts.

It took a while for folks to figure out that I might be for real. In fact, I'd been on the faculty for over five years before an invitation filtered through the pipeline via the deer biologist on our faculty, Dr. Harry Jacobson, for me to come over with him to Palmyra Hunting Club to meet the club's members and to take a look at some of the island's overflow lakes along the Mississippi River. The visit went well, and as we were swapping tales one evening after dinner, I mentioned to my host, Buddy Ball, that we had a new fisheries biologist on our faculty, Dr. Marty Brunson, whom they needed to get to know.

Buddy and the other club members listened carefully as I shared with them some things about Marty: that he'd grown up in south Alabama, had come to Mississippi as a young man to go to college and play baseball and had eventually earned a Ph.D. in fisheries from Mississippi State University, that he'd spent a few years working down at Louisiana State University before coming back to Mississippi State University as our fisheries extension specialist, that his roots in the South and its culture were solid, his heart pure gold, his focus steady, his commitment to friendships and faith unwavering.

After I'd finished, the room was quiet. Buddy looked around the room surveying expressions from the other members of the club. Seeing general agreement he nodded his head and, after taking a sip from his drink, said, "Sure, Don, we'd love to have him over for a visit. How about y'all coming over the last week in October? Does he like to hunt? Squirrel season will be in full swing then, and bow hunting will also be good."

"I'm a squirrel hunter, Buddy. Marty is really more of a bow hunter," I replied. "But we'd come to work. We want to help with your fisheries. I can bring some of my sampling stuff, and Marty and I can give the club an idea about what you've got here and what you can do with it."

"That's fine. We'd appreciate that. But we also want y'all to hunt," Buddy said. "You two need to spend some time rambling around and looking over this island."

Firm handshakes all around sealed the mission.

So it was that Marty Brunson and I found ourselves later that year making our first pilgrimage together to Davis Island. It was the beginning of something almost sacramental to us. We knew that we were receiving a blessing of sorts.

A few weeks later, just after the first frosts had brushed the Mississippi countryside, we drove down to Vicksburg, crossed the Mississippi River over into Louisiana, and then made our way south, deeper and deeper into the river's floodplain and along the river's levee to a ramp on an off chute of the river that served as the island's gateway. There we were met by Buddy and crossed the chute on a private ferry powered by a flatbottom boat and outboard motor over to the island. After the crossing, I found myself once again in some of the most beautiful, wild, southern bottomland hardwood forests that exist in the United States.

The road across the island was rough but passable. It was midautumn and the rains had yet to come. As we bounced along the road, each turn, each bend, took us deeper and deeper into the landscape . . . deeper and deeper into the forest primeval . . . deeper and deeper into the last vestiges of President Davis's old plantation . . . deeper and deeper into something oozing the spirit of the long-gone Confederacy and a way of life, a connection with the land, and interplay between humans and land and river and forest and wildlife and swamp and lake that has all but vanished elsewhere in our country.

Then the woods opened and in the open ground, the last vestiges of cultivated land in the old plantation, were the hunting camps—a collection of houses and trailers perched high on pilings, with a clubhouse situated high on a remnant of an old seventeen-mile-long levee built with mules and slips before the Civil War. In the old fields, crops were planted to provide forage for wildlife. There was an airstrip for club members who preferred to access the property by plane. And there was a quietness . . . a deep rich quietness . . . that enveloped us. It not only played upon the ears. It stilled the heart. The gentle rustling of the wind in the branches of wild pecans around the camp house seemed only to intensify the stillness.

We moved our gear into bunk rooms and then jumped into Buddy's ageing Ford Bronco. Buddy wanted to take Marty to a deer stand for the evening's hunt and said he'd drop me off on the way in an area not far from the clubhouse for some squirrel hunting. After the hunt I could walk back on my own.

After Buddy dropped me off, I walked down an abandoned logging lane toward a slough. There were wild pecan cuttings all over the ground from squirrel activity. There were deer tracks and raccoon tracks, and then I bumped into a whole family of raccoons. I just stood there, watching them scramble around in front of me. The little kitten coons didn't know what I was and were curious. They'd get close, then rush off behind a tree, then peer around it to look at me again. Finally they got bored with the game and bumbled off with their mama. About that time the wind died and I began to hunt. There was only about an hour before dark and I wanted to get back to the camp before then.

I finally got to the slough and started working my way along it. Then, the woods erupted in squirrels. I'd never seen anything like it in my life. They were in that patch of woods by the scores, crashing through the branches, barking, digging in the ground, scratching up trunks, and scurrying along logs. In less than thirty minutes I had seven fox squirrels in my bag. I really wanted to get number eight before leaving the woods but suddenly all squirrel activity stopped. Nothing stirred. It was spooky how fast the mood changed in that woods. I hunted for another twenty minutes without seeing another squirrel. Then, as dusk took over the land, I walked out of the woods and onto the road that would lead me back to the clubhouse.

I enjoyed the walk. It was so quiet. The only sound I could hear was the very distant rumbling of a river boat. The stars were out and the deer were all over the ryegrass and wheat fields. I could see the lights of the clubhouse across a big field. A chill settled over the land. The squirrels hung heavy on my back, and so I took off my vest and just slung it across my shoulder. It felt better that way.

Just as I entered the clubhouse yard, Buddy and Marty wheeled in and there was tension in the air. Marty had put an arrow through a deer, but they had not been able to find the deer. There was blood, but they needed help. So, we all piled into vehicles and went out to look. We searched for over two hours, through brambles and swamps and along creeks and sloughs but were unable to find the thing. Everybody was sick over it, especially Marty.

We were all pretty quiet over dinner but sort of got over it as the evening wore on. We'd all lost deer before and knew that we probably would lose more in the future. Buddy shifted the subject of the conversation and focused on the island's fisheries. The major emphasis was crappie but bass also were important to the club's members. We made plans to collect data from some of the overflow lakes the next day, and discussed how and why this would be done.

Marty and I had a ball sharing with these fine men aspects of our profession and trade. They listened intently and asked focused, to-the-point questions. I think it was then that Marty and I both realized that we were a real team.

Afterwards we poured ourselves drinks and went over by the big fireplace to slouch and visit and tell tall tales. Circling us, all along the walls of the camp's den, were the heads of trophy deer, an old zebra skin donated as a gift from an African safari, some ancient hunting regulations and, on a wall near a big sliding glass door to the outside, an original bill of sale for an African American slave and her young son.

I read that bill of sale, and my heart felt as if it were ripping apart. I felt the pain that flowed across 150 years from that yellow paper. It brought into focus the ugly part of my heritage—that even as we were evolving away from slavery before the war, it was tearing at human souls, black and white, casting a pall over our land and over us.

That bill of sale was on the wall because we don't hide from the truth in the South. That bill of sale was right out there on the wall of the camp's den for all to see. It was there to get right in our faces, to remind all of us that, in spite of our steadfast pride and allegiance as southerners, there was and continues to be the haunting reality that we just didn't move fast enough back then to get things right before the Yankees came. I eased over to a big window and looked out at the land as the light faded. Ghosts were thick.

I walked outside, into the night air. I took a deep breath and then walked out to the road that led back to the woods and the slough where I'd hunted that afternoon. The sky was so deep and clear. There were geese flying overhead, high-pitched calls telling me that they were snows and blues. Their calls comforted me, reminding me that the world is one of eternal drama and change, and that God is, in fact, in charge. I turned back to the clubhouse, joined my friends, poured another drink, and eventually drifted off to my bunk.

The next morning Buddy Ball had Marty and me up before dawn, put sausage biscuits in our hands, and handed me a mug of hot coffee. Outside it was as still as the inside of an empty church. Not a leaf stirred. Marty would bow hunt again for deer. I'd squirrel hunt with Buddy.

Buddy cranked up the Bronco and we were off. In the beam of our headlights deer eased from the ryegrass and wheat that was planted along the road and then faded back into the woods. There were occasional raccoons down by ditch culverts, and twice we saw what seemed to be foxes darting across the track in front of us. We came to Marty's deer hunting area and dropped him off. It was still an hour until sunrise.

After about fifteen more minutes of driving we pulled up to a stop and got out of the vehicle. As the sky brightened I could see small flights of ducks over the cypress breaks and occasional doves flitting across the fields. Buddy pointed to a scope of woods to the left and said that it was for me, and that I should be back at the truck by 9:30 so we could go get breakfast. He'd hunt the woods to the right.

I grabbed my .22 rifle, made sure that I had my compass, took my bearings, and sauntered off into the woods. The dew was heavy on the weeds by the road, but, once in the woods, I had relatively dry walking. Leaves were just starting to fall, but the morning's dampness kept them fairly quiet underfoot. I eased along, keeping to shadows, being careful with my feet so as not to make noise and also—this was very important—so as not to step on a snake. Being an old southern boy, looking out for snakes was just sort of second nature. We learned to do it as kids without interrupting whatever other activity we might be doing out in the bush.

After only about five minutes of hunting I saw the first squirrel, a black fox squirrel, dusky still in the early morning light. On Davis Island one fox squirrel out of seven is the black phase. The others are the orange phase. I let the squirrel scratch around for a couple of minutes in a water oak tree while I settled down for a good steady shot with the rifle. Leaning against a big tree, I held the rifle steady, put the crosshairs of my scope on the squirrel's ear, and squeezed. There was a "whap" as the bullet struck, followed by a "thump" as Mr. Squirrel hit the ground. He kicked a couple of times and was still. I walked up to him, marveled at how black and shiny he was, stuffed him into my game pouch, and started walking along the edge of a cypress break that coursed its way through the hardwood timber.

The woods were amazingly open. The timber was old, mature, and shaded the ground. It was truly the "forest primeval" of the Acadian people (the Cajuns of Louisiana), so well described in the epic poem *Evangeline*. As the sun began to send scattered shafts of light through the forest canopy, the trees suddenly were working alive with squirrels. Branches crashed and limbs swayed. There was a steady rain of cuttings as squirrels worked on acorns and pecans. Occasionally I'd hear the crack of Buddy's rifle in the distance. My rifle was cracking pretty regularly too.

Down past the cypress break I discovered a large grove of wild pecans. Squirrels were absolutely tearing the place up. Most of the squirrels I saw were the orange color phase but there were also a lot of black ones. I didn't bother to sit down and wait on squirrels by feed trees. It was a morning for stalking, a morning for a hunter to test his woodsmanship. And besides, this was new country for me. I wanted to ramble and explore and get the feel of the place.

I drifted from the timber for a little while and explored a tree line along a palmetto grove. Then I melted back into a timber stand that was more cathedral than forest. In that cathedral I followed little twisting sloughs, studied tracks in the mud, occasionally jumped deer and turkey, and side-stepped a cottonmouth. I found foundations from old buildings that I later learned were slave quarters back when the plantation was in operation. Beyond these structures was an old well. I looked down into it and saw movement. It was crawling alive with snakes—mostly cottonmouths but also a few rattlesnakes—that had fallen into the pit and now depended on the small mammals like mice and squirrels that happened to fall into the place with them.

I moved on and on across the island, deeper and deeper into something beyond the land. I couldn't stop.

Something pulled me into the shadows and then into the light, time and time again. After a squirrel or two in an area, I'd just cruise on to someplace else before settling into hunting again. Sometimes I'd just stand at the edge of the woods, scanning the woods across a small clearing until spotting a squirrel, and then seeing if I could make it *across* the clearing rather than around it without the squirrel spotting me.

That morning's venture into President Davis's woods had to be just about the most fabulous squirrel hunting I'd ever had in my life, and the land had to be some of the most tremendous land I'd ever had the privilege of hunting on. It was also some of the most somber. There was something eternal and haunting in that forest. There was a dankness that penetrated my senses. It was like something trying to die and be born at the same time. The wind in the forest swirled. So did the winds of my soul.

When I ambled back up to the truck Buddy took one look at me and at my hunting vest hanging heavy with squirrels, and said, "Some place, isn't it?"

"Good Lord, what a place! But it's more than the hunting, Buddy, it's more than the woods. While I was out there it was as if I could hear voices pulling me on, deeper and deeper. I couldn't stay put. I had to keep moving."

Buddy looked at me hard and then grinned just a little. "They said before you came here the first time that you were part of all this, Don. I guess you really are. You know, this is really all that's left, apart from what's still stirring in our souls."

"Well, Buddy, whatever it takes to keep it, whatever it takes to protect and nurture it, absolutely must be done. And it needs to stay out of the public domain. This place just can't become a park, although there are many who would like to see that happen. This ground is too hallowed for such a thing, not to mention the fact that even if only in the dreams of new generations of southern boys and girls, they've got to know that there still is a place like this that is wild beyond wild, a place where the river commands, where the wildlife is thick, where the forests are dark and primeval, where a man can roam with gun or rod, ramble the trails, drift by boat, hunting, fishing, or just reconnecting with the earth, and know that it belonged to the president of a country, our country, now gone yet still very much alive in all of our hearts."

We ambled over to the Bronco, stowed our game vests and guns, and went to check on Marty. When we got there he was ecstatic. He'd had deer all around him, but they'd all been bucks. Some of the bucks had been dandies. But he'd not shot since he thought he was only to take a doe. Buddy was a little upset about this and said, "Marty, you can shoot any deer you want to shoot. I've already told folks that back at camp. You're right, we focus mostly on does here on the island to keep the population level right, but you're a special guest and you can take a buck if you want."

When we got back to camp, breakfast was ready—thick country ham, eggs, biscuits, juice, coffee, and plenty of Tabasco sauce. After we ate and cleaned up the dishes and kitchen, we went outside and cleaned our squirrels. We'd have them for supper that evening.

Then it was rambling time. We drove down to a place called Cypress Lakes and there we launched a boat. After crossing the main body of the lake, we cruised for a while along a trail through flooded woods and then moved into another part of the system. The trees were magnificent; huge cypress and tupelo gum were out in the lake, and along the banks and on higher ground there were oaks and wild pecans. Alligators and wading birds were thick. There were a few early migrant ducks. Fish swirled. Snakes slithered. Turtles plopped off logs. The outboard motor hummed and churned through the weeds and crystal-clear water.

After exploring Cypress Lakes, we were introduced to a couple of oxbow lakes and overflow depressions that were on the property. The club members wanted to know what really was in them. So, we rigged up some electrofishing gear, worked the lakes throughout the rest of the afternoon, caught a few fish that we processed for fisheries data, and then headed back to the camp house for supper. When we arrived, another of the club's members was in the final stages of preparing squirrel stew.

Buddy took us over to a map on the camp house wall and showed us where we'd been. He was proud of this land and proud to be able to share it with us. The thing that impressed me as we stood there looking at the map was the immense scale of the place. Davis Island is not just some wooded tract of land tucked in some secluded spot along the river, with an oxbow lake here and there. To the contrary, this is an area where hundreds and sometimes thousands of acres are added or swept away every year as the river sculptures the landscape. And those gains and losses are insignificant in comparison to the rest of the property. They're nice to ponder, but they really don't matter. There's so much more than a person can hunt, so much more than a person can fish, so much that a lifetime would really only let you sample the place, like an explorer sampling a mountain range. The explorer knows the general drift of the land and the major features. But there will always be secret spots that will never know a human footstep. There will always be the unknown, always discovery, always a sirens' call . . .

The next morning I did not squirrel hunt but chose rather to accept an invitation by Buddy's sister, Beverly, to fish for crappie in Palmyra chute. Marty would hunt deer again that morning. We planned to leave the island that afternoon, and Marty wanted to grab just one more morning on a deer stand.

Beverly and I fished quietly and steadily with lead-headed white jigs around some upright posts driven into the bottom of the chute for that purpose. There seemed to be crappie at every post. There would be a gentle tug, then a steady pull. If you pulled back too hard, you'd lose the fish because they have such delicate mouths. Beverly, however, was a master fisherman, with just the right touch. She caught two or three for every one that I caught. I'd feel the tug but then pull back too hard and lose my fish.

By the time the midmorning sun was high and it was time to go back to camp, we had an ice chest full of the nicest crappie, nearly all of them "slabs," that you ever saw in your life. They lay on the ice, silvery, speckled with black and green, and in the still air I could smell the wonderful clean rich odor of them, fresh from the murky water. Crappie like that from the Mississippi River have a smell that is like no other fish in the world. I imprinted on it early in my childhood when my uncle Bob and his friend Joel D. Lindley took me fishing on another chute, and when I smell it, it sends me drifting through the years, to other boats, other mornings.

This morning was one of fog lifting from the water and herons drifting overhead. It was a morning so still and calm that the gentle bumping of the boat occasionally against one of the posts seemed to be some sort of insult to the day and the place. We were the only boat on the water. The aura of wildness was overpowering. Nothing here was tame. This chute had in fact once been the main channel of the river, back when the area was President Davis's plantation.

But the river was like our nation. It had had other ideas and eventually shifted its main channel to the east, leaving only a remnant of itself over here as an echo of past glory. Like the old South, it was still deep in places, and there were still ancient scars on high banks where the old river had sliced chunks of land away during former rampages. But now the place was more reflective and somber and, though still moving, realized that eventually it would cease to exist, and then the island would be connected with the mainland, no longer an island, having evolved over time into something else, still beautiful, still good, but fundamentally different.

Truly our currents have shifted, and what once was unique and deep and strong is fading into something else. The sacred island of our southern souls, that island of dreams that stirs our hearts and is filled with shouts of jubilation and anguish, of tears and heartbreak, of magnificence and beauty and victory and subjugation, and acceptance, is an image growing faint. We struggle to hang on to it. We cling to its last vestiges, trying to divert the flow of the main current just a little more so that we can still have a bit of what once was. But we know it is going. We know that a restless land, a restless river, a restless nation, will scour and fill and be renewed, reborn, generation after generation.

I see it in my own children, the new powerful current that blends like never before the souls of the South; and with this blending a new land is coming, a new way, a new heritage . . . a blessing. But the old echoes will still linger as long as there are those of us who have heard the stories from the ancient ones. And it is up to us to be sure that when we pass them along the stories are truthful. "Once we had a way and for some it was beautiful and for some it was horrible beyond imagining. It had to change—we knew that. But we didn't do it fast enough. The ghosts tell us that. They linger in special places just for that reason. And those of us fortunate enough to drift through their realm will be touched, renewed, saddened, strengthened, and filled with visions of a world that was, a world that never could be, a world that is, and a world that will be."

Marty got his deer that morning, and I spent much of the rest of the morning helping him skin and cut the critter, working at the sink in the boot room out by the back porch of the clubhouse, cutting, trimming, and then packing it. But we decided not to take the deer off the island. Somehow it seemed only right that it stay there. So Marty gave it back to the camp, and it went into the camp freezer.

And in that regard, after many years and many visits to the island, I've only taken one thing from it that I can hold in my hand. Buddy and I were scrounging around an area near Gin Lake one December afternoon, looking at old wood from ancient cypresses. The wind was calm. The woods were deep, dark, and wet. The sky was overcast. Ducks whistled overhead. I'd spent the last couple of days hunting deer with my black powder muzzle-loader rifle. I'd seen lots of deer but had, in response to some deep echo in my soul, refrained from shooting. I really don't know what it was all about, but I heeded that echo. Those echoes tend to be trustworthy compasses.

Down along the lake, Buddy and I walked on a carpet of cypress leaves, red-brown, fragile, and soft. Under the carpet was dark earth and in the low areas, it was mud. Sometimes our boots sank into the mud and there were sucking sounds as we pulled loose. It was as if the island was determined to hold onto us, just as we were trying to hold onto it.

After a little while Buddy found one especially nice piece of wood about five feet long from a long-gone monarch and asked me if I wanted it. It was grey with age, weathered, with long creases and ridges along its faces. It was strangely beautiful, smooth to touch and very, very tough. I accepted the gift. I knew what I wanted to do with it.

Now it is in two pieces, one holding the mount of my older son's first duck and the other holding the mount of my younger son's first squirrel. Both boys know that the wood on their mounts is as significant as the critters that are on the pieces. They know the origin of the wood (the tree was probably alive when Jefferson Davis was president of the Confederacy). They also know the old stories as well as those of their papa. They've been exposed to truth, and I think—I think they sense the power of heritage.

It's all I can do. I hope it's enough.

Ptarmigan on Eagle Summit

Interior Alaska stood quiet and brittle, locked in winter's grip. Overhead, the northern lights danced. Weaving and darting, mysterious pastel ribbons of color rippled dreamlike in the early morning hours. To the south, a faint yellow glow promised the dawn of another brief subarctic day.

Winding through the frozen hills in an old pickup truck, my partner, Dean Rhine, and I were on our way to hunt rock ptarmigan on the windswept slopes northeast of Fairbanks. With steaming cups of coffee to knock the chill from our bodies, we quickly settled into the essential elements of a prehunt overture. The conversation drifted, focused and drifted again as new vistas unfolded before us in the half-light. Alaska has captivating powers. Unfinished sentences are a common occurrence here. The vastness of the place can still the soul as well as it stills a conversation.

In the far north there are really only two seasons. There's one called "Friends, Relatives, and Big Game

Hunts" that lasts for about four months and another one generally referred to as the "Real Alaska" that lasts the rest of the year. Once the geese have deserted the land and the rivers have frozen, a different rhythm commands. The trappings of civilization continue to function, but just barely at forty degrees below zero. Life becomes a series of very deliberate actions. One of those deliberate actions is hunting ptarmigan.

There are three species of these northern grouse in Alaska: the willow ptarmigan, the white-tailed ptarmigan, and the rock ptarmigan. In the areas we hunt there are only willow ptarmigan and rock ptarmigan. Willow ptarmigan hang out in the thickets and on windswept tundra. Rock ptarmigan are generally found in the mountains above tree line.

Ptarmigan are noted for changing from a spotted brown and white plumage in the summer to a white plumage in winter. They are hardy birds, equipped with heavily feathered feet (for running away from you across the snow), and, when cranked up into high gear, they can be hard-driving pilots on the wing.

They can also be quite tame if they've had little previous contact with hunters. Sometimes they refuse to fly, preferring instead to scurry around in front of you, snatching buds and frozen dried berries as they go. But with persistence, a naive flock can be put up, and, once shot at, ptarmigan become transformed into the fine game birds they are meant to be.

Ptarmigan are for the most part taken for granted in Alaska, and in fact may be one of Alaska's best-kept secrets. This is not by deliberate intent. It is simply that most serious ptarmigan hunting occurs when people "from the outside" aren't around. Seasons are long and bag limits are liberal. Many are shot with .22 rifles for subsistence purposes throughout the state and often contribute considerably to the welfare of folks living out in the bush. But to those who are thrilled at the prospects of good wing shooting, these northern grouse provide opportunities for tremendous days in the field.

Dean and I pulled off the road just as the sun broke above the mountains. We were on a windswept pass above the tree line. The snow was blown, crusted, and in fact was entirely gone in some spots. We very quickly discovered that the snowshoes we'd brought along with us were not needed.

As we entered the head of the first valley, we were enveloped by the silence so characteristic of Alaska during winter. The wind calmed, and we stood looking out over the sweep of the land. Scattered here and there were stands of low brush and small twisted spruce trees.

Suddenly, far below us in a ravine, we heard a faint chattering . . . ptarmigan! We'd been spotted, but that was what we'd hoped for. The tendency for ptarmigan to chatter gives their position away and helps hunters locate the almost perfectly camouflaged birds against the snow. We advanced slowly in the direction of the chattering until eventually I spotted a lone bird standing out beyond a snow drift near some vegetation. I motioned to Dean and he moved forward.

Without warning, the air was full of whirring white wings. One bird went down at Dean's shot, and the rest of the flock fanned out across a nearby slope. After retrieving the downed bird, faintly pink against the pure whiteness of the snow, we searched for the singles.

Adhering to the ethics of wing shooting, we took turns at shooting as the singles burst from the snow and into the air, one after another. Sometimes we'd spot them at a distance, move into range and, as they rose into the air, which sparkled with tiny ice crystals in the sunlight, we'd take our time with the shots. Taking six birds from that first flock of approximately thirty, we left the valley in peace and entered another one full of hush.

Soon, birds were again filling the air with their cackles and whirring wings. We held our shots to under thirty-five yards and found that with modified and full-choked shotguns, and number six shot, we were deadly. More open chokes would probably have worked well for the wing shooting itself, but would be a liability when we were trying to collect cripples. These birds, once down, will run if they can. On the ground they're tough to kill and can escape if not quickly collected. The importance of a tighter choke becomes quickly apparent after you've been chasing a wounded ptarmigan across a few deep snowdrifts.

We killed six more ptarmigan between the two of us from that second valley and were full of the spirit of a well-conducted hunt. As we began to climb back up to where the truck was parked, a single ptarmigan suddenly launched itself from the base of a spruce and went rocketing over me. Swinging and firing instinctively, I watched the bird fold and plunge into a deep drift. Slowly I worked my way into the drift, reached into the hole and carefully retrieved my last ptarmigan of the day. Placing it gently upon the snow, I knew that this was the end of a perfect hunt. The wind began picking up and afternoon shadows stretched across the snow. In the distance a lone ptarmigan chattered. Below, silhouetted against a grove of dark spruces, a flock of five or six ptarmigan flashed momentarily, then disappeared into another drift to roost for the night.

I whispered to myself, "This is why I'm here. These are the treasures of an Alaska winter."

Turning in the fading light, I started up the slope to the truck, wondering if it would start, but ready to accept the possibility that it might not. Six hours at twenty below zero can suck the life from a battery and turn oil to thick sludge. But I didn't really care. I was where I wanted to be, living the dream. The crunch of boots on the snow, the chill settling in the valley, the awesome quiet, the awesome land, the awesome memories flooded my senses.

A raven called my name, and it echoed through the valley.

Deeper Currents

The Ozark hills were washed with an orange glow as the afternoon sun settled into the valley beyond us. Shadows edged out across the river, and with them came the penetrating chill of late winter. A stillness surrounded us, swallowed us, as our boat drifted with the current. The limestone bluffs above the river clung to the dark side of the mountain, grey-streaked sentinels standing as stolid guardians over all that spread before them. From one of the bluffs an eagle launched itself into the winter sky, its white head and tail sharp and distinct against the blue. It drifted on stiff wings around the edge of the mountain, then was gone, leaving in its wake an awesome loneliness.

I was with my son David. We spoke little, preferring rather to listen to the song of the river and whispers from the land. I steered the boat quietly with a paddle, pausing from time to time to cast toward the bank. David, on the other end of the boat, was casting with a steady rhythm, covering the water before and beside him . . . cast, arch, plop . . . waiting a moment, allowing the minnow-shaped lure to sink to the proper depth, swimming it back to the boat with a slow, steady retrieve . . . prepared to strike back in an instant . . . then casting again . . .

We were on the White River in north Arkansas, about a hundred miles downstream from Bull Shoals Dam. We had the river completely to ourselves. Alone with clear green water swirling all around us and along the rocky shoreline of the river, we were intent on connecting with rainbow trout. But the river, the bluffs, the mountains, the valleys, the day were working their magic on us, connecting us with more than fish.

It was still too early in the season for most people to be thinking about fishing, and much too early in the season for tourists. It also was the middle of the week, and so even the few hardy souls in the area who knew the magic of winter trout fishing were mostly disconnected that day from the river, marking time until the weekend gave them their freedom back. Beyond this, it was too late for the few winter anglers there were that day to still be out on the water. Typically they leave the river before evening shadows form on the hills.

After decades of fishing for trout on the White River I knew that winter fishing could be the best fishing. Beyond the rawness of icy winds and rain, beyond the frozen gear, beyond the stiff fingers and watering eyes, beyond the blizzards were poetry and sublime beauty, hints of unconstrained wildness, larger trout than those typically caught when the dogwoods and redbuds cast their blush on the hillsides, and *much* larger trout than those that swarm in the waters to snatch up worm-draped hooks trailed along the stream bottom by summer tourists.

Cast, retrieve . . . cast, retrieve . . . cast, retrieve . . . then suddenly David's rod bucked and the reel screamed as a trout slammed into the lure. Winter trout not only are usually bigger than those found at other times of the year but are somehow stronger, faster, and more determined, and, for some reason, their colors seem to be much more vibrant than during other seasons. It is as if the winter river conditions them, tightens them up, and stokes their spirit, filling them with some unmeasurable vigor. Winter anglers also tend to respond to the wonders of winter, becoming stronger, tougher, perhaps more colorful, and certainly more introspective than they are during other times of the year.

As the afternoon deepened, the river worked its magic on us—two men, a grey-bearded father in the afternoon of manhood and a teenaged son moving into its sunrise, holding fast to something that cannot be counted or measured, something that connected us to each other as well as to the world around us. The river, the trout, the hills, the stillness and mystery of approaching twilight served as catalysts for powerful bonding, not of the ionic variety with sharp angles and precise arrangements but more of the covalent sort, with blending of natures and mutual sharing of energy elements, beginning with the outer levels and, as the day progressed toward night, moving ever toward the nucleus, tightening the bond at every step.

David's rod, strongly arched and throbbing, pointed at the line that sliced along the surface of the water. My son, a trout angler seasoned already by several years on the river, handled the fish magnificently on the light tackle. After a couple of hard runs that stripped line from the tiny reel, I could see the fish coming, darting in the current, boring deep into the dark water, shaking its head, trying to be rid of the lure that was hooked solidly in its jaw. Even in the shadows there was still enough light to penetrate the water and show the green speckled back and rosy silver sides of the fish.

David called for the net, and I moved into action. As the fish came alongside the boat, I reached for it, surrounded it with the frame of the net, and swung it onboard. The trout came glistening and twisting, an animated jewel from another world, casting a spell of wonder on us that so beautiful a thing could be real.

Cautiously David removed the hook from the fish, then held it up, not as a trophy, but rather as a sacrament, something sacred, pointing to something of a higher order, bridging realms. Then gently he placed it into the live well. We would keep our catch, and consume our catch, thereby letting the fish serve as the pathway for the river to become part of our mortal as well as our spiritual selves.

With a few strokes of the paddle, our drift continued on course down the river, and we started fishing again. Moments later both rods suddenly lurched, and two trout danced on their tails before us. As with the first fish, these were both very fine rainbows, full of fight. The little rods strained as line peeled from the reels. During the fight with my fish I occasionally had to reach for the paddle and give a few strokes to keep the boat from drifting into rocks. When this happened, the fish took full advantage of the situation and stripped off more line or, more dangerously (for the fisherman, not the fish), made a rush for the boat, in the process scaring the wits out of me as the arc of the rod diminished.

David, on the other hand, didn't need to worry about the drift of the boat but had to work his fish to the net alone without my help. That meant that he too would have to handle a hard-charging rainbow for a few moments with only one hand on his rod while his other hand reached for and handled the net.

Miraculously, we managed to bring both fish into the boat. They were gorgeous things, about fifteen inches long, weighing about two pounds each. They were robust, thick-bodied fish with bright colors and finely formed fins. Their eyes glared at us and their gill covers flared. Both were female fish, with fine, small heads and rounded noses.

After putting them into the live well with the other fish, we checked our lines, knots, and lures and continued fishing. We moved on gently along the rocky river bank, our lures plopping into pockets and eddies, slipping along the edge of dark, deep holes, probing ever deeper into the river around us and the currents within us.

We watched as an otter slid into the water and prowled the shoreline for its evening meal. A barred owl called from some deep hollow. A hatch of small mayflies began, and soon was followed by swirls and snaps all over the surface of the river as trout moved in for their dinner. But we knew that, given the choice, these trout would much prefer to chomp down on a wayward minnow than to dart around here, there, and yonder for tidbits of tiny insects. So, we kept feeding our lures to them and they kept on slamming them.

Over the years I've experienced excellent fishing on this river but nothing to compare with that afternoon on the water with my son. Within an hour we each had five of the finest trout you can imagine. They were not the monster lunkers that are known to prowl these waters. Rather they were just fine, healthy, robust, deep-bodied fish—the sort that warm a fisherman's heart and cause him to grin and take a deep breath. We each were allowed one more fish, but both of us refused to fill our limit. We just kept on fishing and releasing the fish as they were caught.

The light faded from the sky. A skim of frost formed on the upper edges of the boat's gunnels. Our fingers stiffened to the point where we could hardly tie the clinch knots on our lures. I avoided rocks in the river not by seeing the rocks but by seeing the ripples flashing below them. Looking upstream I could see lights twinkling in the distance, letting us know that back at the boat landing my lifelong friend Joe Peceny, who owned the landing and boat that we were using, was giving us a beacon to guide us home. I knew that he would not worry about us until half an hour past sunset. The White River is a big river, a powerful river, and at night a very dangerous river. It is not a place to be much beyond sunset. We would have to hustle if we wanted to add the finishing touches to our catch.

I cranked the outboard motor. Pointing the bow upstream, I held fast to the edge of a gravel bar, the boat skimming on what seemed to be nothing. The water blended magically with the night, with the sky, with the world of the never-never. I kept the course, knowing the river, trusting my memory. Then I swung the boat toward the western bank, with water swirling around rocks and the shoreline very dark and growing more indistinct by the minute. Cutting off the motor I felt the current of the river grip us. The boat began to spin but by then I had the paddle in hand and set the course for the final drift and our final fish. David was already casting, and within moments so was I.

But it was all over. The trout were finished. We fished for perhaps another ten minutes without a strike or even a half-hearted bump. Darkness suddenly commanded the winter sky and overwhelmed the river. We reeled in our lines and arranged our tackle without so much as a murmur. Our communications were in a different dimension; we both knew it and were content with it. David drew his jacket tighter around him and pulled his knit cap closer over his head and over his ears. I pulled the starter cord of the outboard motor. The motor was still warm from our trip up the river, and it quickly caught and purred. Gently I swung the boat into the current. We made our way slowly and carefully upstream, past the dark shadows of a bridge over the river, and on to the landing.

Once there we slipped the boat into its mooring at the boat dock, secured it, gathered our fish from the live well and quickly cleaned and bagged them. Fish in hand and souls at peace, and with steam coming as we spoke and breathed in the cold winter air, we walked up the hill to Joe's fishing resort restaurant, gravel crunching under our boots. A grin, a slap on the back, and a cup of hot coffee greeted us as we walked inside.

Later that evening, as we dined on finely prepared steaks, David and I tried to estimate how many trout we'd caught that afternoon. However, we soon abandoned that kind of thinking, realizing that it hadn't mattered then and that it didn't matter now. Beyond the ten that we'd harvested, we might have caught ten more trout apiece . . . it might have been twenty. What *did* matter were our reflections, spoken and unspoken, about the glow of the winter sky, the chill in the air, the murmuring of the river, the arc of the rods, the sparkle of the trout, and the comradery of two anglers alone together on big water. Through our reflections, these were etched in our memories.

After finishing supper I got up to get another cup of coffee, and David walked over to the big picture window in the restaurant. After filling my cup I turned and looked over at him. He stood there, his back to me, tall and straight and so very still, looking out at the dark water of the river that swirled below. I knew that he was back on that river, that his thoughts were moving over the water, and that, at least for these precious moments, his spirit transcended where he stood. I hardly dared to breathe for fear of breaking the spell. My heart was filled with a fullness that only a father knows. Then David turned, saw me watching him, and grinned. At that moment the beauty of those memory etchings was transformed into treasure.

The Irishak Bull

It had been a long Arctic night, with the aurora crackling and snapping overhead while we chased grizzlies away from our camp and the tiny Piper Cub that was parked just beyond the flickering light of our campfire. It wasn't the bears' fault. They were anxious to apply the finishing touches to their layers of fat prior to hibernation.

My Alaskan friends, Dean Rhine, Joe Webb, his son Mike, and I had a camp that flooded the area with wonderful smells: the Dolly Vardens caught from the nearby river that we'd fried up for supper, meat from three caribou we'd shot the previous days, hides from a wolf and a bear shot that afternoon, and all the trappings that hunters bring along with them on wilderness hunts—soap, spices, fuel. We'd tried to do everything "bear wise," cooking away from tents, putting meat and hides off to the side but still close enough to watch and defend. And we realized that the bears probably were curious as much as they were hungry.

But the end result was the same. Bears in camp are not pleasant and cannot be allowed. And bears around an airplane can sever your lifeline and result in a very long walk out. So, we'd thrown rocks, yelled, brandished burning embers, and fired our rifles into the air, trying to convince the bruins that the world was a much better place, at least a quieter place, somewhere else. Somehow it worked, but dawn found us a pretty ragged-out bunch of hunters.

Regardless, there was business to attend to. Moose were on the agenda for the day, and there would be only eight hours of daylight to make it all happen. Winter was closing in. A front was on its way. We had to be packed up and back to the airstrip by the haul road in no more than three or four days or else we stood the chance of getting blasted by the first storm of the Arctic winter.

Years before, I'd hunted down on the Alaska Peninsula and had shot a caribou late one afternoon. So had my buddy Dean Rhine. By the time we'd gotten our caribou skinned and cut up, the sun was setting and a cold wind had begun blasting its way across the mountainside we were on. We didn't make it back to camp that night. There was no moon and walking would have been unthinkable. So, we'd just hunkered down where we were, bracing ourselves, back to back to conserve heat, wrapped in one of those lightweight "survival blankets" that are more of a psychological boost than anything else.

An Alaskan night can be an awesome thing when you have no cover, cannot build a fire because of the wind, and smell of fresh caribou blood. I did not want to repeat that experience up here in the Arctic.

The Ivishak River valley where we were hunting now up on the Arctic National Wildlife Refuge was teeming with moose. The day we'd arrived in the area, Mike, a magnificent bush pilot who flew that plane like some airborne Jeep, had given me an absolutely wonderful tour of the region. We'd flown for a couple of hours low over the flats and gravel bars, and skirted the cliffs and rocky spires of the Brooks Range. Caribou were scattered everywhere on the flats and moving along slopes. Brown bear seemed to be along every stream. Moose antlers flashed from every corner. Fish were piled up, adding beautiful splashes of reds in the deep, clear, green holes of the river. It was a wilderness wanderer's paradise and for me, a hunter deep in my soul, the realization of a long-held dream.

Mike and I finished our breakfast, tidied up camp, grabbed our rifles, binoculars, and day packs and set off along the bluff that ran alongside the river. Almost immediately we began seeing moose. Within a half mile or so of the camp, we'd spotted several, but most were cows or "mulligan bulls" with small antlers. As a non-resident hunter, I was restricted to bulls with antler width greater than fifty inches and with at least three brow tines per antler.

The land sparkled before us in the early morning sunlight. The tundra was ablaze with the deep red of frost-nipped vegetation. Most of the birds in the region had long since departed on their migration south. The land, the day, the quiet—so awesomely huge, a silence, an expanse of vast tundra and sky beyond all boundaries. I could hear water trickle over gravel in the river below me, and the crunching moose two hundred to three hundred yards away as they browsed on willows.

From time to time Mike and I stopped and glassed the valley with our binoculars, looking for a good bull. There really was no place for moose to hide out there on the tundra. Most of the vegetation was shorter than they were, and the bulls' antlers were constant signals flashing across the valley in the morning light.

After a couple of hours of hiking along the bluff, we spotted a decent bull working along the opposite bluff, perhaps half a mile distant. To get to him, we'd have to cross the various braided channels of the river, make our way through the brush unseen, get up on the opposite bluff, above the bull, and circle around behind to cut him off. And all this assumed that the wind would stay still, keeping our scent from drifting to the moose, giving our position away.

I had my Winchester Model 70 rifle chambered in .30-06, and loaded with 180 grain hand loads. It was a faithful old companion of many hunts, with knocks and scratches all over the stock. But those scratches were badges of honor, carefully smoothed with loving care by hand and linseed oil each year after the season. The rifle's barrel had been re-blued on late winter nights at my kitchen sink more times than I could remember, and yet still had that weathered look of an old veteran— more or less still in good shape but sort of blotchy looking when the light hit it just right. Above all, however, was my faith in its performance. It shot true, and with a proper rest, would keep those 180 grain bullets inside a four inch group at two hundred yards. It just seemed to shoot itself. All I had to do was line it up and control my breathing.

Even so, when hunting in Alaska, I always had questions about that gun. I often thought to myself that the hole in the end of the barrel was just a bit too small. But it was too late now to change to something bigger. It was the rifle I had with me, and the old song from my youth in Arkansas started to echo in my mind: "You've got to dance with the one that brung you."

We were able to jump from rock to rock, crossing the river quickly, without slipping or getting our feet wet, and after forty-five minutes or so, had made it through the flat and on to the base of the opposite bluff. From there we couldn't see our bull, but figured that he was near to where we'd seen him at the beginning of our stalk, so pressed on up the side of the bluff.

Once on top we had a problem. The sun was now in our eyes when we looked back across the river flat, and there was a lot of glare when we tried to glass the area with our binoculars. Additionally, we were skylighted on the crest of the bluff. So, we backed away from it and made our way toward the bull sort of by guess and by gosh, trying to estimate where we were in relation to the rest of the valley and the bull by the position of a large, rocky hill off to the west.

When we thought we were just about right, we got on our knees and crawled to the edge of the bluff for a peek. At first we didn't see anything so we just stayed put, looking. Then, off to my right, I saw the bull, about sixty yards away, hooking his antlers in some willows and occasionally snatching a mouthful to munch on. He looked fine, dark and huge, standing in the willows, his legs fading to tan, his shoulders humped, muscles flexing beneath the skin, a big bell dewlap hanging under his neck, and antlers still rosy red from having recently shed their velvet.

I shucked my day pack and jacket, stuffed four extra bullets into my hip pocket, and was about to begin sneaking up on the beast for a clear shot when some motion to the left caught my eye. About fifty yards away, lying down, was another moose, a bull we hadn't seen when we'd made our crossing. I couldn't see the whole animal, but his antlers were huge and towering above the brush he lay in. Occasionally, I could see an ear twitch but that was all. Lord, but did he have big antlers! They looked like a pair of dining room tables perched up on top of willows.

I quickly altered my plan. I motioned to Mike to come have a look. I heard him gasp and whisper, "Buddy, that dude is a monster!"

We then started slithering along the ground like a couple of snakes, getting closer and closer to the bull. We got so close, in fact, that I could hear the bull breathing and a rumbling from within his chest. We got to perhaps fifteen yards from him when Mike tugged at the cuff of my hunting pants and motioned that we should stop. Quite frankly, I thought we probably should have stopped long before, but had just kept on crawling from sheer momentum and adrenaline. But as I'd gotten closer and closer, I kept thinking about that little hole in the end of my rifle's barrel and about how ugly things could get if that bull decided that we didn't belong in his world. At a body weight of eighteen hundred pounds or more, an Alaskan moose is the largest deer in the world, and he also has the meanest temper.

We just lay there, breathing, trying to get ourselves calmed, trying to think of all the things that could go wrong so that if they happened, we'd already have worked out our plans. The main challenge now was that we still couldn't see anything except antlers and an ear, and he was sort of lying at an angle away from us.

I got up on my knees, quietly slid a round from the magazine into the chamber of my rifle, and took a steady position. The bull still didn't know I was there. The sounds of his breathing and that rumbling in his chest seemed deafening to me in the quiet. But how was I to get that beast to stand up so that I could shoot?

Mike whispered, "Clear your throat."

I cleared my throat but only got an ear twitch in my direction.

Mike whispered again, "Well, clear it again!"

I did, and eighteen hundred pounds of bull moose stood up right in front of me!

Quickly I put the crosshairs of my 4X scope on him, but all I could see was brown hair! I couldn't really tell where I was pointing. I was too close for the scope to be any good to me. There simply was too much animal there to shoot at. I was looking at a target about the size of a tool shed at a range of less than fifteen yards now. So I looked over the scope, across the end of my rifle barrel, then, looking through the scope, traced the back edge of his foreleg down to the heart-lung area. Mike was whispering hoarsely, "Shoot! SHOOT!"

And I squeezed the trigger.

The rifle bucked; the crack of the shot sounded like a cannon, with echoes reverberating across the tundra hills. The moose just stood there, then turned his head in my direction, saw me, laid back his ears—and I shot again. He still stood there, even after having just received two .30-06 bullets in the boiler room. But after that second shot he started walking off, through the willows and along a mucky, sloshy tundra trail, his rear end and antlers the only thing visible to me. It seemed that he was picking up steam and speed in spite of being shot. Mike brought up his rifle and indicated to me that if I didn't shoot him again, then he was going to start shooting. We had to get that moose down!

I watched as the bull moved into a thick patch of willows and then, just as he came out from behind them, at about forty yards, he turned and gave me a quartering shot. I put the crosshairs on his neck and fired.

Lord, what a sight—eighteen hundred pounds of bull moose doing a complete flip over onto his back, hitting the squishy mud of the trail so hard that I could feel the ground shake, and sending water and mud flying twenty feet or more into the air.

I knew that I had to get up to that moose quickly just in case he was able to get up again. But somehow the moose had crossed a creek down in the willow thicket after my first shots. What's not much of a creek to a moose can be an obstacle to contend with for a man. I finally found a narrow spot after a couple of minutes of searching and jumped across, only slightly wetting one boot, but not caring.

When I got up to about ten feet from him, I saw him down, now on his side, breathing heavily in spite of two chest shots and one in the neck, and with his eyes riveted on me. I could tell that he was watching me approach, and when I got nearer, he tried to kick me with one of his back legs. He darn near succeeded too!

I jumped back, took careful aim on his neck just where it joined his skull and administered the coup de grace. He kicked twice and then was still. Blood filled the wet tundra trail. The echoes of the last shot faded into the hills. The quiet returned. And I had my moose.

Lying there on that tundra, he was much bigger than he'd looked when I shot. Those antlers were absolutely magnificent, with six long brown tines on each fully pal-mated antler and an antler spread several inches beyond my full reach, at least seventy-two inches. He was more than magnificent, he was gorgeous—big Roman nose, bristles along his back, hooves the size of dinner plates. He was a bull for the record books and perhaps the best that had ever come from this part of Alaska. I really couldn't believe it. I'd have been happy with the first moose we'd stalked. He had been a real dandy. But this big fellow on the ground before me was a dream come true.

Now, the work began. A moose is not dressed like some whitetail deer down in the South. You don't roll a one-ton beast over on its back and slit it up the belly. You just start at the top and work your way down. You lay back the hide as you go and when you get something clear, you cut it away. It took us two hours to get half-way through the moose to a point where we could get at the huge mass of lungs, heart, liver, and digestive tract. I more or less crawled down inside the beast, cutting and heaving, until finally, with Mike's help, we were able to roll it all out and to the side next to the first rack of ribs, shoulder, and a six-foot-long backstrap. Then we split the hide along the top hind quarter down to the hock and began peeling it away until we had it almost clean. Working with my knife, I sliced and dug deeper and deeper into the meat until I was able to find the joints at the hip and hock. I cut and cut and cut, until finally the joints were separated, and then I sliced everything free so that we could hoist the 150-pound hind quarter up and out of the way, huffing and heaving, over to a rack of willow branches we'd prepared for its bed. Then we trimmed off the remaining pieces of meat, about fifty or sixty pounds of it, put it into a cloth game sack, laid it beside the hind quarter, and started working on the other half of the moose. In another two hours, we had another shoulder, hind quarter, rib rack, and backstrap up on the willow rack. Then we turned on the neck, head, and antlers. Mike started carving off neck meat and putting it into another game sack. I started sawing at the antlers with my pack saw. It took me more than an hour to get through the hide and skull and then, pulling forward with all my might, leaning on the antlers, twisting and grunting, finally breaking them free. They must have weighed nearly a hundred pounds. So, in less than five hours, we had our moose processed—somewhat of a record from what I understand.

We were about a mile from our camp and didn't have backpacks with us to haul out the moose meat and antlers. We'd have to go back and then make plans to return the next day for the stuff, knowing full well that chances were very good that by the time we got back, grizzlies would have moved in. But there was nothing else we could do.

When we got back to camp we found that Dean and Joe also had taken a moose, but it wasn't more than two hundred yards from our camp. It was a good bull, at least as big as mine in body size but with very different, more branching antlers without much palmation. They had it cut up and ready to haul out by the time we arrived. We spent the rest of the afternoon and early evening getting it back to camp.

The next morning, Dean, Joe, and I hiked back to my moose while Mike got into the plane to scope out the situation. He'd check to see if grizzlies were on the kill and then let us know by wing wagging. He circled low over the spot, and came back wagging like some red and white butterfly. We had trouble ahead. By law, bears have priority on kills. They cannot be shot unless the hunters have the appropriate tags, or the bears attack. We'd already taken two grizzlies on this hunt and I didn't have a tag for another. But bears usually will not attack unless pushed to defend their prize, and so, a bear on your kill probably means that you will not be able to claim your kill.

We moved cautiously toward my moose while Mike continued to monitor the situation overhead. Somehow, however, by the time we got to the kill site, there were no bears around. One rack of ribs and one sack of meat was missing, but everything else was intact. All three of us had backpacks and into each was loaded either a hind quarter or a shoulder. Then came the hike back to camp with our loads. You go step by step, enter into a sort of other-world consciousness, cross the creeks, find openings through brush, on and on and on, pack frames creaking, pack straps cutting into the flesh of your shoulders and rubbing your waist raw until, finally, the camp comes into view. Then lunch, a hike back to the kill site, another load goes into each pack and back to camp; you are bone weary, but have a song in your heart. Then, back for the final load and the antlers. In Alaska, the antlers cannot be brought out until all the meat is back in camp. It's a good law. I carried the antlers; Joe and Dean brought out the last of the meat. We got back to camp with our final loads just as Mike started setting out plates for supper. Fresh moose meat, biscuits, gravy, and beans. I think I ate five pounds of moose.

This was my first and probably will be the last *big* bull moose I will ever shoot. One size extra large in a lifetime is enough. If ever I'm so fortunate as to be able to go back to hunt in Alaska, any moose I shoot will be of the smaller sort. There is certainly the practical side of the matter, moose for meat, the packing out of the beast, etc., but then there is also another dimension.

The grandeur, the magnificence, the absolute awesomeness of this huge moose really has left no room for another great beast of his sort in my memories. His antlers grace the wall over my fireplace, broad, deeply palmated, long tines reaching out across the room, massive bases slightly sagging where the weight of the antlers during development took their toll, and forever take their toll on me also, taking me back again and again, as my mind swirls and my heart yearns, to the land that I love so much.

Especially on quiet winter evenings, when I'm alone before the fire, with the lights dim, after my kids are in bed, my wife moving gracefully around the house, putting things in order for the night, the flames casting primeval shadows and flickers throughout the room, I look up at those antlers over my fireplace and Alaska reverberates in my soul. I am full of the beauty of it all, the vastness of it all, the lonesomeness of it all . . . it stirs me so deeply, with echoes unending. I drift off to that faraway land beyond the Brooks Range, where the aurora shimmers overhead, where the grizzlies prowl, where the char flash in streams, and where bull moose thrash the willows and each other with their antlers. I can feel the bite of the wind, see the slopes of distant mountains, feel the crunch of frozen tundra under my feet, see once again the flash of antlers catching the morning sun on the other side of a braided river, hear the tinkle of ice drifting on currents.

I also feel something swell within me, something powerful, something so right, something that transforms me into another man, the different man that lives only there, the one that becomes fully what he was intended to be, senses sharpened, muscles somehow given power that comes to them like this in no other place in the world, a different sort of power, a smoothness, a relentlessness, a boldness, and a mind so clear, a heart so full of song that I just don't need another big moose. The one I took works his magic without any help at all.

Winds*

I came to the Stikine's raw wildlands,
　　Where the marsh grass and tides sway and swell
I came for the rain, cold and slashing
　　Where the whispers of wings cast their spell.

The teal and the mallards and widgeons
　　Cupped their wings around the pond where I hid,
Dipping and swirling before me,
　　Fulfilling the dreams of a kid.

But it wasn't the shooting that mattered,
　　And it wasn't the ducks that fell.
No, there was something else there that gripped me:
　　Alaskan winds had their messages to tell.

I listened awhile to their discourse,
　　And I felt my heart tug at its roots.
The sirens were calling—I knew it.
　　And I pondered the weight of my boots.

But other songs were heard off in the distance.
   There were also winds there quite well known.
A wife and three kids can work magic,
   Even two thousand miles from my home.

So, tonight I go back to my family,
   Alaskan blessings upon me once more.
But quite frankly I'm far beyond ready
   For the hugs "Papa" gets at the door.

*Composed while returning from an Alaska duck hunt

A Deer Hunter's Journal

DATE: 23 November 1997

DEER # : 25

DESCRIPTION: Mature doe

LOCATION: My farm, Oktibbeha County, Mississippi

GUN: Winchester Model 70, .30-06

BULLET: Winchester SuperX 150 gr. bullet

Deer season opened yesterday (Saturday). In the past few years since I bought the place, my farm has become very good deer habitat. I've groomed it, nurtured it, and protected it. There are quite a few deer that call it home. Earlier this fall I hunted with bow and arrow, saw deer during nearly every hunt, but didn't kill one. Conditions have to be just right before I draw my bow on a deer, and somehow things just never worked out that way.

But I anticipated a fairly quick and efficient hunt once gun season opened and made plans to get the venison I wanted into the freezer this opening-day weekend, and then get on with the serious business of duck hunting. I usually need three to four deer to last my family of five for one year. Getting two or three of them early in the season would take some pressure off me.

Opening day was foggy and still to begin with. I got on my stand overlooking my "quiet corner" about 5:30 a.m. Barred owls were hooting, ducks were whistling overhead, and night critters, mice and stuff, were scratching around. With the dawn came a north wind, only an occasional gust of five to ten miles per hour, and a steady breeze of two to three miles per hour . . . perfect.

Squirrels started coming out everywhere—big Bachman's fox squirrels, with black faces and white noses. I even had some of them up in my tree stand with me, scratching around the bark, pushing their faces close to mine, trying to get me to blink. Below me was my green field planted with ryegrass and wheat. Beyond the green field was my old corn patch with a few dry, sad-looking stalks still holding ears. The tree I was in was a post oak in its prime, dropping beautiful acorns everywhere all around me. Deer had discovered those acorns as well as the green field and were hammering them. From where I sat I also could see back into the woods about fifty yards. All I needed was a deer.

But a deer did not come. With the exception of lunch, I sat in that stand all day and saw not a hair. In fact, for an opening day I was surprised at how little shooting I heard. I enjoyed the day, however, watching a pair of hawks soar above my woods and a great blue heron nail one of the catfish in my pond.

Today was a repeat performance of yesterday except that the weather was even more perfect for deer hunting. There were birds of all sorts: thrushes, brown creepers, a pair of tiny ruby-crowned kinglets (in my stand), flocks of robins, white-throated sparrows, blue jays, and all sorts of woodpeckers. And of course the woods were alive with squirrels. I sat and sat and sat, watching my beautiful farm drift through the day. The light played on the trees, casting a spell on them and me. Slowly I linked my spirit to the land and became as one with it. Perhaps that was the secret.

Once I shifted from a deer harvest perspective to one of union with the spirit of the land, the magic came. I began to see and hear more. I breathed differently. I sent my spirit out into the woods searching for the deer, and then started pulling them to me. I felt the force of the pull, worked it gently, careful not to break the bond, and at twilight, the witching hour, the shuffling of hooves upon leaves came from behind me.

I glanced over my right shoulder and saw a doe. She was about thirty feet away and moving steadily toward the patch of green field in front of me. I could hear another deer behind her, but my focus was locked on that lead doe. The rifle came up smoothly, as if it had a mind of its own, crosshairs settling on the deer, tracking her through the brush, waiting for the perfect clear shot that the spirit whispered would come.

The doe entered an open spot, turned, and presented me with that perfect shot. The rifle bucked and the doe was on the ground. She bleated once, kicked twice, then was still. I quickly turned back to look into the woods where I'd heard the other deer, and there it was, drifting back into the shadows. But I did not raise my rifle. The spirit had already whispered to me that the hunt had ended.

A beautiful doe had been given to me in a powerful way. I sat in the tree stand for a few minutes, breathing slowly as stillness returned to the dusky woods. A chill began to settle on the land. Night shadows grew deeper. Stars came out. The owls returned to sentry duty. Then, taking a deep breath and checking my rifle to be sure it was unloaded, I climbed down from my stand, checked the deer (she was bigger than I'd first thought), then walked back across my land to my truck. It is a trek, a hunter's trek, that I've done so often with other deer, and always I make it with a sense of peace, satisfaction, humility, thanksgiving, and a bit of sadness. The mixture is a good one.

The drive back across the pasture, headlights bouncing, the sight of the deer, still and beautiful on a carpet of crushed leaves, the heft as I pull the deer into the bed of the truck, field dressing the deer beside the pond, washing hands and knife, pulling the deer back into the truck, rambling across the wooden bridges that span my creeks, the closing of the gate to the farm, listening to the crunch of gravel . . . transition back into the other world, but never the same, never the same.

Baking the Bread of Life

(A Scoutmaster's Reflections)

It has been a cold night. There is frost on the tents and on the withered grass where the troop has camped. It is still . . . so still . . . but as the first rays of sun slip past the branches of the winter woods, turning the world into a sparkling fairyland, there is the ring of an ax on wood. In every troop there is a boy whose instinct calls him to be the fire tender. Another boy crawls from his tent, hair tousled, bundled in a puffy red scout jacket. He begins to poke around inside the patrol's cooking kit. Except for these two, there is no activity in camp except that of the scoutmaster. The other boys are still curled in their sleeping bags. As the scoutmaster makes the rounds from tent to tent, checking on the boys, his coffee mug in hand, he can see small bundles inside, cocoons of a sort, with puffs of steam slipping out of the breathing holes the boys have made by tightly pulling the drawstrings of their sleeping bags around their heads.

There is crackling as the fire gains strength. Two old Dutch ovens have been pulled from the cooking kit and now sit beside the fire. The two boys work as a team. They have the responsibility for preparing breakfast for the other scouts, and in so doing they will pass off a requirement for their next rank.

They know that the other scouts will be hungry. Yesterday's hike to the campsite, the games that took them out through the dark woods on a nighttime compass course, and the cold of these early morning hours will produce shortly a pack of howling, ravenous hyenas who must be fed before they become boys again.

Flour and water are mixed, dough is prepared, and globs half the size of a boy's fist are placed into the Dutch ovens. A hole is prepared in the fire so that the Dutch ovens can be placed on the coals. More coals are placed on the lids of the ovens. It doesn't take long before the aroma of baking bread drifts through camp and into the tents. There is stirring in the tents. Slowly the other boys come out of their tents and gather around the fire. A few of the younger boys, on their very first campout, poke sticks into the fire, trying to get a higher blaze, but a stern warning from the twelve-year-old cook gives them direction to keep their sticks away from the ovens. There are bisquits baking. It is in many ways a timeless scene, with echoes coming from the far distant tumbling generations of humankind. These boys are hooking up to those echoes.

Baking bread. For untold thousands of years we've taken grass seed, ground it into a powder, mixed it with water, and stuck the mixture into ovens of all sorts. And for untold thousands of years, we alone among species have captured the power and art of fire making.

Thus, baking bread is truly a distinctly *human* activity that links us simultaneously to heaven and earth, and to each other. Baking bread is a conduit through which energy that has been transferred from the sun to the grasses and trees, and stored in plant tissues, is brought into our lives as food and heat. Baking bread is also a conduit through which spiritual energy is passed in fellowship. To break bread with someone is more than just eating. It is a linkage, a bonding, a union that has sacred overtones.

When a scout says, "Please pass the biscuits," he's seeking absolutely, and in no uncertain terms, to tighten the bonds of brotherhood with his fellow scouts. And when those biscuits are passed to him, the bonds with those other scouts are in a very real way confirmed and strengthened.

One of the old songs of the Boy Scouts' Order of the Arrow begins with the words "Firm bound in brotherhood, gather the clan . . ." and goes on to say "circle the council fires, weld tightly every link."

We focus now on the baking of another type of bread, baking the bread of life through scouting. We take these gifts from God, our youth, both boys and girls, carefully shape the loaves through the Boy Scout and Girl Scout programs, fan the flames of adult leadership, bake the loaves in the ovens of schools, churches, and community (and while these young'n's bake they fill our lives with their distinct aromas), ensure that they have just enough crust so that they can keep their shape and protect their deeply held qualities, and then share them with the world.

This baking bread business requires focus, discipline, and work. We must till the fields; plant, cultivate, and harvest the grain; produce the flour; and gather energy from various sources to make our fire. It is an eternal process. Without it we have no future. The quality of the bread we end up with depends on the investment we make in it. We can wrap dough on a stick and get by, or we can prepare the coals, prepare the ovens, handle the dough with the reverence it deserves, and produce something, perhaps a boy or a girl, that glorifies God. Jesus knew the power of bread, symbolically and literally. Bread in both dimensions is central to our humanity, and a reflection of our immortality. As Jesus proclaimed, bread is truly our link with God.

When Jesus spoke to the crowd along the lake shore he said, "It is my Father who gives you the real bread from heaven. For the bread that God gives is he who comes down from heaven and gives life to the world . . . I am the bread of life. He who comes to me will never be hungry." And so in scouting we bake this bread by emphasizing reverence for God and respect for God's creation. We bake the bread as we work to equip boys and girls with a sense of ethics and a solid foundation of competency and self-confidence that will endure for a lifetime and beyond through selfless giving. We wrap the programs in action: camping, hiking, canoeing, travel, adventure.

But always there is the underlying scouting mission: serving others by helping to instill values in young people and, in other ways, to prepare them to make ethical choices over their lifetimes in achieving their full potential.

Baking the bread of life . . . the values addressed in the process are wrapped succinctly in the Boy Scout Promise: "On my honor I will do my best to do my duty to God and my country and to obey the Scout Law; to help other people at all times; to keep myself physically strong, mentally awake, and morally straight."

And what does it mean to "obey the Scout Law"? Well, this is what the Scout Law says: "A Scout is trustworthy, loyal, helpful, friendly, courteous, kind, obedient, cheerful, thrifty, brave, clean and reverent."

Jesus went on to say, "And it is the will of him who sent me that I should not lose any of all those he has given me." This is also our mission in scouting—that we will not lose any of those given to us. I'm not talking about the kids we lose in the woods from time to time. Those lost sheep are eventually found or they eventually come wandering back to camp. When we find them they're generally making it just fine; they were trained in what to do out there. But I'm talking about the others, the boys and girls that we miss, kids that don't receive that positive touch in their lives that scouting gives. They are the kids that are our concern. To make the bread we want to make, we need those kids. The fire is just right now and the oven is ready.

There is power in bread. Bread is a blending of the gifts of God through the work of human hands. It warms us, energizes us, fills our senses; it draws us close to one another, around a campfire, around a table, around the table of the Lord. When we share bread with one another, the same earth elements and the same energy from the sun are distributed within us. We become one in body and, through our fellowship, one in spirit.

Overture to Christening a Magic Wand

When you've fished for half a century as I have, some stuff begins to sort itself out. I'm not what you would call a hard-charging fisherman. I despise fishing contests, because in my opinion they demean the fish and the fishing. Fishing is not a competitive sport. Rather it is a contemplative one. I was fortunate to grow up before fishing tournaments and powerful bass boats polluted the waters. I could take a canoe out on a major reservoir or large river and be alone. There were a few other fishermen, but they operated at a scale that was unobtrusive. We all caught a lot of fish and some big ones too. We didn't have to churn the water to a froth doing it, and we didn't depend on electronics to find the fish. We read the water and the weather and that was enough. We fished slowly and thoroughly. And it made a difference.

Fishing became so deeply ingrained in our psyches that it became art as much or more than science. We operated on hunches and intuition and thoughtfulness.

Our tackle was pretty simple also. We moved quickly through our childhood gear, mostly cane poles, and as soon as we'd saved enough money, usually bought some sort of spin-casting gear. Some of the old men still used level-winding bait-casting reels with braided line and leaders. Most of us kids didn't like that stuff because it took time, experience, and skill to cast without a back-lash. The spin-casting gear gave us more time to fish. There were some kids with real, open-faced spinning tackle, but we considered them aristocratic snobs for the most part. Usually their parents had bought their tackle for them. Most of us got our tackle by saving trading stamps or running paper routes.

And the same went for tackle boxes and lures. We'd go to the sporting goods stores and drool over the lures. We knew what we wanted and saved hard for them. They were investments: Heddon, Arbogast, South Bend, Rebel. We took care of them too. During January and February, after the hunting seasons had just about run out and before fishing really kicked in, we'd spread all our tackle out on newspapers in our bedrooms, sort it, clean it, sharpen hooks, touch up paint, check guide wrappings, disassemble, clean and oil reels, and wax and rewrap rods.

About the time that we entered high school, most of us had also picked up a fly rod. But our fly fishing wasn't for trout. In fact, our trout fishing back then was limited to a Boy Scout trip or two each spring, far away (about three hours) in the Ozark Mountains. We fished for trout like we fished for catfish—bait on a tight line, fished on the bottom. *Our* fly fishing was for bass and sunfish, and typically it kicked in after the major spring fishing was over and the water had warmed enough that we could wade and swim in the lakes. Although I sometimes fly fished with friends using a boat, my normal fly fishing was pretty much focused on wading around the shore of the lake near my house, sometimes with a popping bug and sometimes with what we called a "bream killer." A bream killer was just a bit of chenille or pipe cleaner wrapped around a hook, and then some rubber band legs were tied on to make it look like a spider. Mostly I used black, but sometimes yellow or green worked.

My rod was big and cumbersome, but I didn't know the difference. It was a nine-foot-long salmon rod, and it had a Pfleuger level-wind reel. My great-uncle Earlie Calvert had given it to me. He was a dedicated fisherman and had traveled all over the United States on fishing trips. Since I'd never met my grandfather Jackson (he died when my father was thirteen years old), Uncle Earlie, my grandmother's youngest brother, filled that part of my life. He loved that role too. He'd take me out to his shed and go through tackle and usually give me something. One time he picked up a three horsepower Johnson outboard motor and handed it to me. I thought he wanted me to put it someplace else and asked him where. "In the trunk of your dad's car. It's yours." I was stunned. And I still have that old motor. I used it to conduct research for both my master's and Ph.D. degrees in fisheries. Although it needs a little work, it still runs, forty years later.

But the fly fishing . . . I'd wade slowly along the shoreline, working the little pockets, catching small bass and sunfish, pretending that they were salmon and trout in some faraway pristine waters. Sometimes I'd catch big bass with that fly tackle. "Big" for me back then was a bass that weighed three or four pounds. It still is.

When I went off to college in north Arkansas after high school, my fly rod stayed home. I didn't fish much at all for a couple of years and I didn't hunt either. I had a wonderful time those first two years, but studying kept me close to campus. I probably didn't fish more than a handful of times prior to my junior year. But then I met an English teacher who introduced me to creek fishing with ultralight spinning tackle for smallmouth bass. That captivated me completely and the fly tackle just kept on gathering dust—for about thirty-five years.

During that time I became more and more of a recluse when it came to fishing. My disdain for the crude culture of tournament bass fishing grew to disgust, and I began also to recognize that the reservoirs were killing the rivers that I loved. I drifted further and further into the shadows of fishing. I went where others didn't go. I fished for fish others didn't want. I used techniques, even commercial gear, that got right up in the face of the so-called "sportsmen" who seemed to dominate the collective identity of angling.

Tiny creeks and ponds became the focus of my angling, while the big rivers were the focus of my profession in fisheries. People just couldn't understand what I was up to. It was easy. I just wanted to be as far away from those folks and their fishing as possible.

After a few years I was able to buy a farm, and there was a pond on it. It wasn't a big pond, just a little more than an acre in size, but it was mine. When I got it, it was a phenomenal catfish pond. I enjoyed it that way for five or six years but eventually wanted something more. I wanted to have water that was clearish green rather than chocolate muddy. I wanted to cast to fish with artificial lures rather than sling bait out.

Finally, five years ago I converted the pond to a bass and bream pond. I wanted to create my own fishing water and manage the entire affair just the way I wanted to. And that pond was tucked back into a corner of Mississippi in a place, in a way, that nobody, except me and a few other folks I introduced it to, would know what was going on.

As luck would have it, about the time I made the conversion, Mississippi entered an extended period of extreme drought. The pond dried until about all that was left was a narrow half-moon-shaped pool along the pond's levee. Although winter rains helped some, the pond never filled its basin during a three-year period, and with the onset of summer each year, the pond would dry up again. The fish population languished and so did the angler.

The exposed pond bottom was baked so hard by the harsh summer sun that I was able to drive my old Dodge pickup truck across it. And I did just that for one entire weekend in July during the second year of the drought, hauling load after load of smooth pea gravel out to three spots I'd marked for fish-spawning beds. At each spot I shoveled the gravel out of the bed of the truck until I had gravel four inches thick spread evenly in an area approximately twelve feet wide and twenty feet long. After three years of drought the rains returned, the pond filled, and the spawning beds were flooded by water not quite three feet deep. The fish responded beautifully.

Because the pond is just a tad larger than an acre, it is just barely large enough to have stable predator-prey dynamics between the largemouth bass and the bluegill and redear sunfish I stocked in it. In fact, because of its size, it is really just a sunfish fishery and the bass are there just to keep the sunfish from overpopulating. A few bass can be harvested from time to time, but you have to be very careful not to tip the balance. If the sunfish ever get the upper hand, restoring balance naturally through bass predation is as tough as the dickens.

My management program keeps the bass population slightly crowded, lean and mean, and subsequently the bream are constantly under pressure. Those bream that survive, those that slip through the vulnerable sizes, pop into a pretty good world as far as sunfish are concerned. There's lots of food and relatively little competition for it. So, they grow rapidly, and when the water is the right temperature, they spawn profusely.

It didn't take the bream in my pond very long to find those gravel spawning beds I'd made during the drought. In fact, they were on those beds almost immediately once the pond had filled and the temperature

bumped the eighty-degree mark. Because the fish population in the pond had suffered during the drought, the
first year that the pond was back across its entire basin
I didn't fish, but I could see the bream swirling in the
water over the beds and I could hear the bass late in
the evening attacking their prey. The following winter,
while setting out decoys in the pond for duck hunting,
I walked over the beds, and they were a mass of fish
nests, little saucer-shaped craters dug out and fanned
clean by the bream during spawning.

Last summer I started fishing for the bream. I wasn't
really serious about it but rather just took my kids to
the pond with fishing poles and crickets. We usually
just fished from the pond's levee rather than taking our
little boat out to fish around the gravel spawning beds.
But we still caught lots of bream and occasionally bass
(which we released). The times we shared were wonderful family times, and I was for the most part satisfied
with the whole enterprise.

By the middle of June, however, I found it increas-
ingly difficult to recruit a fishing partner on the home
front. My kids had caught enough fish, or so it seemed,
and had other interests to pursue. So I drifted into the
mode of the solitary angler.

It wasn't the fish but the fishing that I needed.
I needed sanctuary and sacred time to collect myself
and restore my energy. The farm and particularly the
pond provided both. Out there I could listen to silence
and watch the sunlight play across the surface of the
water. I wasn't really interested in going into town for

bait, however, and so began taking along that old fly rod left over from my childhood days. It was crude and heavy and unbalanced. The reel was rough and warped and had the wrong-sized line. But I didn't care. Digging around in my old tackle boxes I found some worn-out and frayed flies and a couple of rusty eyelets that allowed me to attach a piece of monofilament line to the fly line. The whole rig was enough to make even average fly fishermen groan. But it was all I had and so that's what I used.

I hadn't used a fly rod since high school days. So when I tried using that old gear, walking along my pond's levee, my technique was horrible. I couldn't get the timing right, and my wrist just wouldn't move like it should. The line would get all tangled up at my feet and the old reel would bind and stick.

But bream are a forgiving sort of fish. Even with my poor equipment and technique, they started sucking up the flies that I presented to them. That old stiff rod didn't give the fish a chance to fight much, but regardless there was a special connection between the fish and me that traveled along that rod. I could also feel the pulse of the fish through the line that I held in my left hand. It resurrected something, some dimension of an old self that I'd forgotten about. It was a sort of magic. I was transported back into that former dream time I'd had as a youth. The bream would tug and spin in circles and then come splashing and sparkling across the water to me. They were as big as my hand and as round as a saucer. They were broad across the back and thick and firm on the shoulders. Their sides were almost irides-cent, some dark and reddish, others more golden, fading to silver underneath. They were jewels in every sense of the word.

I kept the fish I caught that afternoon, about ten of them. When I got home, I cleaned and filleted them and realized that for a decent fish fry, I'd need some more.

The next day was Sunday. After church I went back to the pond, again alone, but this time I took a cooler with cold drinks and a cushioned boat seat. I hauled my little boat out from its spot back in the woods and slid it into the water about thirty yards from one of the gravel spawning beds I'd constructed. This would be a different approach, a different challenge. I'd be sculling with my right hand and fishing with only my left hand, working the shoreline rather than working *from* the shoreline. It would be tough with that heavy old rod, but I was determined.

It took me a while to get my old rhythm back. It seemed to flow from somewhere deep inside of me, but once it was all reconnected, I entered into a beau-tiful sort of fishing that absolutely touched my soul. The little boat responded to the slightest touch of the paddle in the water, and the line from the rod started moving back and forth, tugging just right on the back cast and laying that fly up against the bank or beside a stick or into a tiny pocket with hardly a dimple. Those scrappy old bream absolutely tore that fly up. They'd suck up that bug and then tear out into the deep water, tugging and spinning and pivoting and then, yielding, come splashing up into the boat. I'd quickly unhook them and shove them down into a wire fish basket with a spring-hinged lid and then keep on fishing. After a couple of hours of this I realized that the basket was getting full of fish. I hoisted it onboard, dumped the fish into the bottom of the boat and realized that I'd caught nearly fifty of the nicest bluegill and redear sunfish you can imagine.

The bream bit the bug and the bug bit me. I couldn't get enough of it but knew that I had to meter myself. I had to let the fish in the pond recover from the fishing. So I started working in a sort of cycle. I'd fish once a week, usually on a Saturday or Sunday afternoon, and harvest around thirty fish each time I went. For about six weeks the fishing never slacked off. I'd work the shoreline and those gravel beds, fill my basket and then go home, so full of the fishing bug and the fly fishing bug in particular that I became a nuisance around the house. I started looking at fishing equipment catalogues and dreaming of owning one of the fine rods and slick reels that were advertised in them. But I hesitated to invest. This stuff, the good stuff, was dreadfully expensive. The price of a good outfit, even average gear, was about ten times more than the value of the gear I fished with. If I was going to do this, it had to be done right. It might only happen once.

Well, some things are just meant to be. I was working at an event for one of our state conservation organizations and mentioned to a friend that I was really enjoying my fly fishing on the pond and was considering buying a new rod and reel. He suggested that, instead of buying a rod out of a catalogue, I go visit with a mutual friend of ours, Tommy Shropshire, a retired wildlife biologist, and see if he would build a rod for me. I knew that Tommy was a fanatic fly fisherman, but I had not known that he built rods.

I talked with Tommy, and he suggested that I take a look at a couple of rods that he'd built, and then we'd talk about the project. When he showed me his rods, I fell in love with them. They were beautiful, light to the touch, glowing with mellowness under the lights, all the parts perfectly fitted as if they were made for each other (which they were). My hands started to tremble, and I dropped one of them. No damage was done, but Tommy recognized how severely the bug had me in its clutches.

Then he began to show me the catalogues that sold the materials needed for building a rod. I quickly realized that the price would be about like those I'd looked at before. The difference would be that I could design the rod to my specifications. That's exactly what I wanted to do.

Tommy and I struck a deal. Rather, Tommy said he'd build me a rod for the fun of it and I'd just pay the costs. Over the course of the next few months we settled on what we wanted, and Tommy started work. It would be a Sage feather-light two-weight rod, eight feet, two inches long, with nickel-silver hardware. One of the main features to consider was the material for the handle. I wanted it made of something very special.

I either wanted wood from out on my farm or something with history or tradition in it. Finally I worked the choice down to two pieces: a piece of Osage orange from an ancient fence post given to me by Dr. Warren Thompson, the former dean of the College of Forest Resources at Mississippi State University, or a piece of seasoned walnut from the original stock of my grandfather Jackson's old Remington shotgun. Family triumphed.

The rod was commissioned in August, and it was the end of January when Tommy told me that it was finished. During that interval I made a trip to Arkansas and found a fly fishing shop with the reel that I wanted. As I waited, I would on occasion reach from my desk to the drawer where I kept the reel and pull it out, crank it a couple of times, and dream of the day when it would be on that rod.

The rod was delivered last night, not in some office, not in some city, but way out in the woods, in a very fine hunting camp, with firelight flickering and good rich talk filling the evening. Tommy handed it to me and I was like a high school boy fumbling through his first date. I was afraid to touch it . . . almost. I joined the pieces and held that lovely tool, that piece of art, lightly in my hands. It is a rod for many lifetimes and will be catching fish long after I'm gone.

Today is cold. I spent the night at the hunting club, down between Natchez and Vicksburg, but left at 4:00 a.m. to drive home. As the day dawned I saw ice around the margins of ponds I passed along the way. I got home at 7:30 and I've had a fire in the fireplace going ever since. It is not a day for using a fly rod for bluegill on my pond. But still I had to go . . . I had to feel the rod move in my hands. I had to feel the tug of the line and sense the line shooting forward through the guides. I had to hear the click of the reel. I had to stir the visions of fishing yet to come.

So, I bundled up, loaded up my rod and a few flies, and drove out to my pond as the afternoon sun cast its glow on the pasture. The fish did not cooperate. They're "iced down" still, hunkered in some deep spot of the pond, waiting, and I'm hunkered down in my own deep spot, also waiting. February is always this way; it is a tough time for an old fisherman like me. It is a month for remembering, so they say, and perhaps that's true. But for me it is really more a month for waiting and brooding and cleaning reels and sorting tackle and checking rods and reading fishing stories and trying to keep from going mad and biting myself as anticipation builds.

But, in about six weeks (assuming I survive), perhaps a week or two earlier if I'm lucky, about the time the chimney swifts return to Mississippi, and the robins are building nests, and dogwoods and redbuds are blooming, and gardens are getting tilled and planted, and turkeys are gobbling, you very likely will detect a faint smile on my face and a certain lightness to my step. You may find a bream killer or two on my desk with the rubber legs chewed off of them, and perhaps a popping bug by my coffee cup that's had all the paint knocked off of it. There may be a wad of old leader on the dash of my truck, and if you look closely you may see a certain roughness on the ends of my thumbs. I may seem distracted and sometimes hard to find. When you observe these things you can be pretty sure that there are three gravel beds out in a small Mississippi pond with bream swirling all over them, and that I've been waving a new magic wand over those waters in a special sort of way.

Reunion

The open door of the smoky cast-iron wood stove allowed the flickering of the flames to send a shimmering golden glow around the room. Books and notes lay scattered in a semicircle around the stuffed chair before the fire. The broad arms of the chair, frayed and showing the matted cotton beneath the fabric, served as a resting place for the half-filled coffee cup. Through the window, the stillness of a mid-November sunset filtered into the room and settled upon my heart. Taking the coffee cup, I stretched a bit, then got up to look through the window and out across the dark Ozark hills that surrounded me. It really wasn't cold outside. The fire was more for atmosphere than for warmth. In fact, the low flame dancing on the logs made the room just the other side of comfortable. I needed a breath of fresh air. More than that, I needed a few moments to stretch my eyes and my mind. Clear winter skies are good for doing both.

Walking through the dark shadows of the room and into the tiny kitchen, I opened the door and walked outside onto the porch and into the open air. I just stood there, quietly, meditatively, letting myself slip into the rhythm of the night.

How deathly still it was. Far across the valley on a distant hill a barred owl called, but rather than breaking the stillness, it only seemed to intensify it. Somewhere, down along the river, a hound struck a hot trail.

"It's probably a coon," I thought, as I listened to it fade away out of earshot.

An afternoon wind had cleared the dust from the mountain air, and in the absence of the moon the stars seemed to hang almost within my reach. Deep inside of me there was a stirring. It was something I savored. It had a flavor which was strong and commanding, yet, from past experiences, I knew that the afterflavors which would bubble up as it simmered and brewed were the ones which would touch my hunter's soul with the richest of bouquets. And so I stood there, allowing the echoes of years past to swirl up from a place where they'd been resting for a while.

I'd been gone from these mountains for three years. Two of those years I had been in Southeast Asia as a U.S. Peace Corps volunteer, and the third year I had been in seminary up in Kentucky. Hunting and fishing had been relegated to a back burner during these sojourns. But now I was back, not only in the Ozarks but on Woolsey Mountain, one of my favorite hunting grounds in the headwaters of the West Fork of the White River. There had been a little spike buck I'd seen on the mountain when I'd left three years ago, and I wondered if he was still around and what he might have become.

I'd come back to the Ozarks as a graduate student in biological sciences at the University of Arkansas, trying to resurrect an old path leading to a career in academics. My day-to-day world kept me close to the earth and allowed me opportunity to spend large chunks of time on the open water of lakes and rivers, working the nets and other gear necessary for my profession as a fisheries biologist. It was a good, solid lifestyle. It gave me opportunity to explore my professional discipline and gave me time to move beyond professionalism, beyond the bounds of society and civilization and into the world of the wild. There was now a deep stirring of energy within me whenever I was out rambling in these hills. My mind would soar and my heart would swell as I prowled the land and waters that I'd come back to. I was, in many ways, a resurrected man.

Surrounded by the stillness of the November night, I focused on the magic of a hunter's world. Tomorrow would bring with it the opening of the deer season, and my mind and body pulsed with anticipation. The thrill which rose again and again from deep within me, passing upward along my spine and finally centering in the middle of my soul, let me know that I was tuned in on the right frequency. A smile creased my face as I turned to go back inside the house. The night whispered a promise. With the dawning of a new day, treasures would be waiting.

Back inside the house I set about getting my gear ready for the hunt. In the corner, leaning against the wall, was my rifle. The light from the stove played upon the rich wood grain of the stock, and flashed softly on the old brass fittings of the leather sling. My movement was something spontaneous as I reached for it. The heft of wood and steel, the smooth rhythmic "click-clack" of the action working, the sharp images of the sights, the smell of light oil and leather dressing, and the ever-so-faint lingering odor of old gunpowder filled my senses. The crisp clean-cut checkering in my grip seemed to steady my hold and make firm the union between man and tool. Power, purpose, destiny lay not with the man or the rifle but in the fluid harmony which linked them together.

Returning the rifle to its corner resting spot, I surveyed the other items that were necessary for the hunt. Leather boots, worn but sturdy, the belt knife with blade now beginning to wear thin with the years, rope, vest, ammunition—it all lay ready for me spread out on the floor beside the stove. Satisfied that nothing was overlooked or forgotten in this prehunt ritual, I unzipped the sleeping bag on my bachelor's bunk and crawled inside. Sleep came quickly, lacking the fitful wakefulness of youthful excitement but warmed by the glow of an anticipated reunion.

I woke up before the alarm clock could shatter the morning's silence. The house was cold. There was steam in the air as I breathed. Dressing quickly, I started breakfast and made some sandwiches for a midday meal in the woods. I wasn't in a hurry, but excitement, now building in anticipation of a reunion with an old self, kept me from lingering very long over a second cup of coffee. Filling my thermos and grabbing my rifle and gear, I tromped off through the darkness to the aged and rattling Rambler station wagon that my grandfather had passed along to me when I'd returned from the Peace Corps.

A slight nip was in the air. There was frost on the newly fallen leaves. The hills lay silent and black under the gaze of Orion. Snow geese high overhead cackled and gabbled, unseen and haunting as they winged their way across the hills.

Cranking the engine of the station wagon and giving it a moment to warm, I began running through the possible plans for the morning's hunt. I'd scouted the area while squirrel hunting earlier in the season and knew the trails, scrapes, and rubs. Although I'd tentatively settled on a spot and a plan the previous day while making a last-minute check on the mountain, with the dawning of this new day there was some hesitation. Something just didn't seem right about it all.

After backing out onto the county road, I drove through the darkness trying to sort out this emerging internal conflict. It wasn't far to the place where I planned to hunt, but in the fifteen minutes it took me to get there, a new decision had been reached. I decided to abandon my former plans. They would have stationed me in a good spot where the likelihood of seeing a buck was very high, but the spot, good as it was, was too close to the haunts of other hunters. It also was too close to a road, and I had no desire to spend the morning listening to trucks and cars rumbling along the gravel as they crawled up the steep hillside.

There was simply more to hunting than taking a deer. So, locking the station wagon, I walked off in the opposite direction, one which would take me far into the hills where I could spend the day reconnecting with the ridges, the ravines, the hollows and creek bottoms of Woolsey Mountain. Perhaps I'd bump into that buck I'd left there three years ago.

I'm not a rambling sort of hunter. Rather, I hunt by selecting a spot and settling into it for hours on end.

"Let the others tromp the brush" is my motto. "As for me, I'll blend into the forest and watch the trails."

I knew this country well, the dips and rises, the old fallen trees and solitary standing sentinels. In the dark I moved along the dry slopes, hardly needing the flashlight, careful not to walk along the trails that the deer were using.

Making a broad arc, I looped back upon a spot that rose above a wide wooded flat. Just beyond the flat but within rifle range was the only crossing of a deep ravine that sliced the slope of the mountain into two sections. The only "dead" area would be behind me. It was full of boulders and was very steep. In years of hunting this mountainside, I had never seen a deer in that area. I had, however, several deer already to my credit from the area which lay generally below me. Maybe, just maybe, that buck would drift through it.

Eventually, I located the bent oak tree that I was looking for and which would serve as the base for my stand. Although it was still dark, I stood for a long time gazing out across the forest which was swallowed in black. I couldn't see much, but in my mind's eye I knew what was there. The rock pile, the tiny spring seepage from between the rocks, the old den tree which always had a squirrel nest or a racoon in it, the clearing, the trail from the ravine . . . it was time to settle and let the predawn blackness swallow me up also.

Leaning against the tree, I loaded my rifle and checked the safety. Then I became very, very quiet. Nothing stirred. I could hear the blood as it rushed through the vessels beside my ears. Slow and rhythmic, it seemed to set the pace for breathing. With heartbeat and breathing now hand in hand, it was a simple step to orient the thoughts into a synchrony with the pulsations. For several minutes I focused on this synchrony until slowly the spirit of the hunter that had stirred the night before began to creep out and take command of my oversoul. My senses sharpened and my mind soared.

The scurrying of woodland mice became almost obscenely loud in the stillness. They were digging, gnawing, dragging tiny pieces of sticks and leaves; it seemed incredible that creatures so small could make so much noise. It wasn't, however, that they were noisy. It was rather that they were the only creatures breaking the stillness.

Then an owl hooted on the hill across the valley, and a coyote began to yelp. Perspective was regained, and the mice could barely be heard at all. Another flock of geese flew overhead. Straining to catch a glimpse of them, I noticed the faint beginnings of dawn just starting to take the sharpness from stars low on the eastern horizon. Though sunrise was perhaps still an hour away, the magic of daybreak had already started. I could now see the outlines of trees nearby and with the passing moments was able to expand my visual range. Shapes and forms loomed and faded and then were transformed into solid objects. The owl still called. The coyote was joined by another and another until a short symphony arose. Someone's dog, now taking notice of his wild cousins, started barking, and that only intensified the coyotes' teasing.

Overhead a crash caused me to look up in time to see a squirrel going airborne as it leaped from one tree into the maze of tiny terminal branches of an adjacent hickory. It was as yet not light enough to tell if it was a grey squirrel or a fox squirrel but from experience I figured that it was probably a grey. Fox squirrels have a tendency to be a bit lazy and sleep later. It would be unusual to see one so early.

I noticed now, while looking up through the branches, that the sky was a blue-grey. Slowly the shadows were being chased from the mountains. The mice no longer stirred. The coyotes ceased their calling. The owl was silent. The squirrel had long ago scurried out of sight and earshot. The quiet once again took command in this final interlude between night and day. The sanctuary-like stillness became thick and heavy, forcing me ever so slowly to shift my weight and wiggle my toes. The hollow drumming of a red-bellied woodpecker echoed through the stillness and was quickly followed by the heavy wing beats of a pileated woodpecker as it skimmed the treetops.

A crow cawed, then another joined it, and then another and another until the woods was full of raucous noise making. I figured that they had discovered some poor creature to harass. Sure enough, before too long, silhouetted against the dark slope of the mountain across the valley, I could see an owl, probably the one I'd heard earlier, being chased by the crows.

The owl had no mind for a fight that morning, bitter enemy of the crows though he might be, and from all appearances, he only wanted to be left alone to sail away in peace. But the crows were relentless in their pursuit, diving and pecking, making life miserable for him as he swerved and dipped to avoid their onslaught. The noise of the fight drifted deeper into the valley and was eventually lost among the hollows and ridges.

Other birds, now active, set about their morning foraging. Chickadees, titmice, creepers, and an assortment of woodpeckers flitted and darted among the trees, pecking, probing, and scratching. Though a naturalist by habit, I tried to filter the focus of my senses through and beyond the supporting characters of the morning's drama.

I needed to be the hunter, completely, fully, totally. I forced a discipline as I engaged the world around me. I listened to it, "felt" it, with single-minded purposeful-ness. Ears sharp to pick up the lightest twig snapping, eyes easily drifting across the field of vision before me, senses relaxed yet intent, ready at any instant to con-centrate on a flicker of movement or the smooth liquid flow of a browsing animal, I became no less the predator waiting for ambush than the bobcat that I knew also prowled this sector.

The day brightened without a whisper of wind. The sun boiled from behind the mountain, flashing pure and crisp upon the forest and the man. Squirrels were scurrying and crashing now all around me, seemingly oblivious to my presence. Red-tailed hawks soared far above in the azure sky and screamed their high-pitched wilderness cry. Among all sounds in the mountains, it was this call of the hawks that was my favorite.

For a few precious moments I broke away from my focused discipline as a hunter and gazed at the bird soar-ing with broad outstretched wings, a dark stripe across its breast. I felt that I was almost able to transfer my soul to that hawk, and see these hills which I loved so much from far above—the crystal green streams, the grey slopes, the shining bluffs with dark mineral streaks, range upon range of folded hills sweeping away into infinity and all within reach of an effortless soaring flight.

Then, drifting back to earth, I checked my rifle and looked around me. How I did love this spot. Old memo-ries rose in my thoughts. There were memories of for-mer hunts, of other deer, of the different moods which had over the years possessed these almost enchanted slopes, of the rain, snow, storms, icy winds, and baking sunshine, of hunts shared with others and of hunts made alone.

My reflections deepened. I thought about what the path had yielded during my years as a solitary sojourner, and how it was expressed in the way I hunted. While others hunted this morning in groups or organized clubs, I preferred to keep to my vigil alone, quietly, independently, and with a profound sense of communion with a world apart from humans. My "hunt" in its broadest sense was not a game or a sport. It was to me a way of life. I liked it this way. I liked being able to move quickly and lightly. I liked backpacks, boots, rifles, worn passports, and challenging assignments in remote and distant places. I figured that man was by nature a hunter and a nomad, and that while shelter and security were nice on occasion, to spend a lifetime seeking or trying to hold on to them ran against the very grain of that central core of my human rhythm. I had no wish to build or to maintain any structures or any "empires" which would inhibit direct, free, communal expression of my true identity as man and creature. I was owned by no man and shared no absolute allegiance to any institution. I was not afraid to die and subsequently not afraid to live. I did not shun risk. The sting of battle was something I rather enjoyed.

A shadow flickered and was followed by a tiny flash of reflected sunlight. My internal dialogue was immediately swept away as my attention riveted upon a spot fifty yards from me through the trees. Hardly daring to blink an eye or even to breathe, I sat motionless while the image solidified and became a large whitetail buck picking his way cautiously down the slope.

I thought to myself, "Could this be what has become of the little Woolsey buck that I saw on the mountain before I left to go overseas? Man, he's become a real dandy!"

The buck was alert but not conscious of my presence. With swollen neck and flashing antlers the deer slowly drifted past a rocky slide. His muscles rippled. Dry leaves crunched under his weight. Closer and closer the buck came toward me, veering toward the crossing which would take him across the ravine.

I saw that there would be only one moment when it might be possible to take the buck without being noticed. Thirty yards away was an old walnut tree behind which the deer would pass if he maintained his present course. I would have to wait until then, when the deer's vision was blocked momentarily, before I could bring my rifle up without startling the buck and causing it to bolt out of my life forever.

Step by step, the deer edged closer until finally, for perhaps two seconds, its head was behind that old walnut tree. That was all I needed.

Up came the rifle, solidly and smoothly. The next step brought the buck back into the open. Instantly, I held the sight on a spot just behind the deer's foreleg and fired.

The buck was knocked to the ground by the impact of the high velocity 150 grain bullet, and then he started sliding across the leaves down the slope of the mountain. After sliding about ten feet he crumpled against a boulder and lay still. The echo of my shot drifted through the valleys and bounced along the faces of the limestone bluffs.

I quickly worked the bolt of my rifle, knowing all too well that a deer can suddenly, and without warning, overcome initial shock and escape. I stayed where I was, ready, waiting, covering the fallen buck with my rifle for two to three minutes, until I was sure that it was down for keeps.

Then I got up and slowly approached the buck, rifle at ready. But I need not have worried. The buck lay very, very still on the crushed leaves of the November woods. The smell of gunpowder still lingered in the air as I bent close to the deer inspecting the shot. A neat little hole was the only evidence that the deer had been struck. The bullet had come apart inside the deer, as it should have, delivering the shock that had brought the buck down so quickly.

Reaching down, I grabbed the heavy antlers in my hands and pulled the buck away from the boulder and to a level spot not far away. I stood there, breathing deeply, slowly pulling the mountain air into my lungs. It was only then that I allowed my heart to pound with the excitement of the hunt and the kill. I grabbed the buck's antlers once again, held my rifle high over my head with my other hand and, like the hawk which had soared over the mountains that morning, I uttered a free-flowing, haunting, wilderness cry that burst forth from the depths of my soul. Its echo drifted off through the mountains, and the mountains sent their messages back to me.

And when I shut my eyes, when I still my thoughts, I can hear the echo once again . . . the Ozarks are all around me . . . that wonderful buck is at my feet. I can almost smell his musty sweetness. It only takes a moment to be back.

Tara's Treasures

Boots stomped on the wooden porch and steps as hunters gathered in the predawn darkness, coffee mugs and sausage biscuits in hand. Labrador retrievers made the rounds, tails thumping against the hunters' legs and cased guns that were leaning against the porch railings, and secretly accepting tidbits from the biscuits. The guides of Tara Lodge checked licenses and made small talk about guns, weather, and the dove field that had been prepared for the morning's hunt. There was a general sense of festivity in the air as the Mississippi Wildlife Federation's board members spoke about past hunts and prospects for the one at hand. Then a little girl dressed in camouflage, with her golden hair pulled back under a hunting cap, drifted into the mix.

"Good morning, Anna," they said, sometimes reaching out for a hug, sometimes to tussle the bill of her cap, as she moved among the hunters and guides, sipping on her orange juice and munching on a sweet roll. She was no stranger to the group or to the place, but rather a veteran with three of these hunts already to her credit, even though she was only nine years old. She accepted hugs from the hunters and guides and face lickings from the dogs as she made her way across the porch to me.

"Papa," she asked, "how much longer until we load up? Do you have enough shotgun shells? You sure did shoot lots of them last year. Where's your gun? I need to go to the truck to get my hunting seat. Are we hunting in the same place we hunted last year? Where's the bug spray? Whose dog is that? Do we have to go home when the hunt is over? Mr. Callahan sure does have a pretty gun. Look at the way the wood glows in the light. I wish we could live here." Although she was still very young, Anna knew that she was already a full member of this hunting tribe.

As the hunters continued to gather, getting their gear ready for the hunt, and while I was engaged in swapping a few tales with old friends, Anna darted off to check the fruit jars that held the tree frogs she'd captured the previous evening. Assured that they were in good shape, she ran back to me and told me that we'd better hurry or we'd be left behind. I told her that we were in fine shape but took her in hand, walked down to the truck, and unloaded our hunting seats and my old shotgun, a couple of boxes of shells, a small cooler (which we filled with ice back up on the porch), and a can of bug spray.

Then the guides started cranking up the hunting trucks and telling folks it was time to begin loading up. Each truck had a canvas covering over its bed and wooden plank seats inside for hunters to sit on. Anna and I picked one of the lead trucks, climbed onboard, and scrunched down on seats between other hunters.

Anna had a big grin on her face. The bumpy ride in the dark out to the dove field was all part of the ritual, all part of her memories, all part of the growing excitement in the heart of a little girl about to meet the sunrise on a Mississippi dove hunt with her papa. Although she still wasn't big enough to carry a gun and shoot, she could be part of everything else. In fact, the other hunters, along with the hunting guides, had reminded her that the most important jobs on the dove field during a hunt were those of spotter and retriever. Although dogs were important and generally had better noses than little girls for finding dead birds, little girls hunting with their papas were able to spot doves for their papas to shoot at, and generally did a better job of retrieving doves than the dogs could because little girls could spot where the birds went down after being shot (assuming that any birds actually *went* down after a shot), and direct their papas to where the birds hit the bushes or tall weeds.

It took about fifteen minutes of bouncing around in the truck to get to the sunflower field that had been prepared for the hunt. Strips had been mowed and disked so that there would be open ground for doves to land and feed. Once in the field the truck we rode in stopped about every two hundred yards to drop off a hunter. Near one of the corners, the driver said it was our turn. First

I grabbed the girl and swung her down to the ground. Even in the grey predawn light, I could see little puffs of dust as she stomped in her tennis shoes away from the truck and over to the edge of the sunflowers. Then I went back to the truck for the gun and gear, waved to the driver and the other hunters, and shuffled over to my hunting partner.

Anna had already made herself a little nest of sorts back in the sunflowers. I handed one of the folding hunting chairs to her, and she started to settle in. I moved about ten feet away from her, set up my chair, arranged my gear and shells, and then took my seat.

There was absolutely no wind at all. In fact, in the stillness I could hear the quiet conversation of hunters on the far side of the big field where we were hunting. I could hear the sound of men loading guns and setting up their chairs and buckets to sit on. As the grey sky began to brighten into the pale blue of a new day, I also could hear the whistle of wings, dove wings, as they whisked across the field. Occasionally, overhead, I could make out the shadow of one of the doves, and even in the half-light, could see the faint pink of their breasts.

About that time one of the guides tooted the horn of his truck, announcing that it was legal shooting time. Almost immediately there were shots, and with the shots, doves began flying everywhere. For a few minutes it seemed that all of the shooting was happening over on one corner of the field along a big ditch. I began to wonder if any would venture our way. Then Anna whispered loudly, "Papa, here they COME!!"

And come they did. Like a hive of bees turned loose, doves were swarming all around and over us. My old pump gun started speaking and about every second or third shot, a dove would crumple in a puff of feathers, fold and auger itself into the ground, or flutter, glide, or pinwheel down into the sunflowers. Doves down in the disked strip were quickly retrieved by Anna. Those down in the sunflowers were my responsibility, with Anna serving as benchmark and navigator and me as the retriever. Within the first hour we had nine birds wrapped in a plastic shopping bag and placed on ice in our little cooler. We were allowed six more birds before reaching the limit. But by then the dawn flight had tailed off, and only an occasional dove came within shotgun range.

So, we just sat there on our stools, hunkered down in our patch of sunflowers, a grizzled old papa and a pony-tailed young'n, watching together as the world came to life in the Delta. We could hear the sound of cotton pickers and combines droning with a deep resonance that seems to still the hearts of those born to this land. Just beyond the treeline bordering the field on its north side, wood storks flew up out of a huge oxbow lake that once upon a time had been the Mississippi River. A flock of Canada geese gabbled and honked in the distance. A tight flock of blue-winged teal buzzed a mudflat over by the ditch. Dragonflies danced among the sunflower stalks. Occasionally, one of the other hunters would shoot. Occasionally, we'd get a shot. The sun popped up over the horizon, a dusty orange thing that looked like you could reach out and pluck it from the sky.

Then, after a shot by one of the other hunters, there was a shout. "Hey, y'all! A rattlesnake has my bird and it's halfway ate!! Any of y'all got a camera?!" Half a dozen men shouted, "I'm on my way!" (It's not every day you get to see a rattlesnake eating a dove, and the pictures came out great—in fact, for some of us, *too* great, too *close*.)

Then the quiet returned and with it came the heat of a September morning. Anna and I sat there, discussing the fine art of wing shooting. From time to time a dove would come whistling by and I'd shoot at it. After a little while Anna sort of skewed her mouth off to one side, wrinkled her nose, looked around at the pile of spent shotgun shells all around us, did a bit of mental calculation (adding up the doves in our cooler—there were twelve by then) and then, in a not-so-quiet voice, turned to me and asked a very serious question. "Papa, look at all those empty shells. We only have twelve birds. Why can all the other hunters out here hit birds with their guns when they shoot at them and you can't? Is your gun broke?"

Sound travels very, very far on a still September morning. And, from near and far, from all around the field, I could hear hunters laughing. There was only one answer to a question like that.

"Dear daughter of mine, I only shoot at the hard ones."

"Why are all the other hunters laughing, Papa?" she asked.

"It's just the way these hunters, these *friends of mine*, have of letting you know how much they respect your papa's skill with a shotgun."

Two doves flew by just then. I missed them both.

The sun finally began meaning business, and one of the trucks slowly started making the rounds through the field with cold drinks. A few of the hunters were finished, either limited out or burned out, thirsty or hungry, and were climbing into the truck as it passed. When the truck got to us, the guide asked if we were ready to go.

"No, sir," Anna replied, her feet firmly planted in the dust beside the driver's window. "We have dead birds lost in the bushes. We need your dog."

Few men hesitate following stern words from determined women, regardless of the age of the woman. Out came the retriever, along with a couple of other hunters. Within five minutes, three dead birds were found in the vines and tangles over on the far side of our disked strip. That completed our limit of fifteen birds.

Anna was thrilled.

"My papa got his limit of birds. Did you get yours?" she asked another hunter.

He just grinned and handed her a cold bottle of water as she climbed up into the bed of the truck and found her seat. The dog, hot from working to find those last birds of mine, jumped up into the bed with us and went directly to Anna, slobbering all over her as she stroked his head and ears.

The truck had barely parked back at the lodge when she and the dog were out of the truck bed and gone. I unloaded our gear and took it to my pickup, then tromped up the stairs to the porch and on into the dining hall for a cup of coffee. Cup in hand, I went out through the big glass doors to the porch, turned the corner at the back of the lodge, and walked along the trail to the pond. I figured that Anna would be there, and I was right.

She was standing on one of the fishing pier's benches, pole in hand, tense, watching a small cork bobber that quivered in the water next to a brush pile. Suddenly, the bobber ducked under the water. With a quick jerk, a hand-sized bluegill came splashing across the surface and up onto the pier. Immediately, Anna pounced on the fish like a cat. I got there just in time to help her take the hook out of the fish's mouth and put the fish into the wire basket that she had tied to one of the pier's posts. There were three other fish, including one small bass, already in the basket.

About that time a call came that brunch was ready, so we stowed the fishing gear and joined the hunters as they lined up for the biscuits, sausage gravy, scrambled eggs, grits, coffee, thick slices of ham, juice, and an assortment of fruits. Our motto was: "If you must indulge, indulge as a warrior." And we did.

After brunch, some of the hunters began to pack up and leave. But Anna pleaded with me to stay—just one more afternoon, just one more night. And it was magic.

Sidney Montgomery, a longtime friend and one of the wildlife managers of Tara, overheard her plea and came up to us, inviting Anna to go with him on a reconnaissance trip around the plantation. Then, as if by afterthought, he looked at me and then back at Anna and asked if she thought I might want to come along. She sort of cocked her head and said, after a long, dramatic pause, "Well, yes, I guess we could take him along."

So, off we went on our adventure, back along the main levee of the Mississippi River, then across the levee into the *batture* lands, over rickety wooden bridges crossing sloughs covered with duckweed and creeks oozing mystery, into primeval bottomland hardwood forests, and on through wetlands, cypress breaks, and tupelo gum swamps priming themselves for migratory waterfowl yet to make it down to Mississippi. Anna sat high in the seat of the pickup, between Sidney and me, straining to see over the dashboard, soaking it all in. Deer ran across the gravel roads and dirt tracks that we followed. A wild turkey, neck stretched and body leaning far forward, trotted down the road in front of us for a few yards before disappearing into the trees.

From time to time we'd stop the truck, get out and just stand . . . looking, listening, feeling something, some force, some power, something undescribable, surround us, envelope us, stir us. The air was thick and still. The forest resonated with the humming of insects and the calls of pileated woodpeckers. Anna would wander away from us, not too far, but far enough away that she could feel something all her own. She'd stand in the twilight of forest shadows and look straight up through the branches, to where the sun was bright and the sky a deep blue. She'd reach out and touch the trunk of a huge oak, feeling the bark and sometimes wrapping her arms around it just to sense the magnificence of something so old that still lived. There were tracks of all sorts in the muddy spots. She'd bend low and follow their trace with her fingers. Small frogs chirped and jumped into the safety of puddles as she walked beside them.

She didn't need a "never-never land" or a "fantasy island." She was in a *real* wonderland, and even as young as she was, she made it clear to us that she knew this. She'd turn and look back at us, smile, and then turn back into precious moments of connecting with the awesome wildness that surrounded her. Some places have just the right blend of magic, mystery, and class to capture the heart of a young'n blazing her trail into the world of things wild and free—the world of hunters and naturalists, adventurers and explorers, where eternal drama unfolds, where spirits lurk and songs swell in your heart, and memories swirl, and you can hear your name being called by the wind as it brushes the tops of ancient trees. And then she'd come back to us and stand beside us, looking out through the forest and beyond, sharing the quiet, letting it penetrate.

"Anna," Sidney said as we drove slowly in the old truck through one of the more remote sections of the plantation, "I want you to know that anytime you're here, honey, Tara is all yours."

She looked back at him and whispered, "Yes, sir, Mr. Montgomery. I know that. You tell me that every time I come here. When I'm bigger, I'll help you take care of it. I'm a Mississippi girl."

Then she put a tiny hand on his shoulder and gave him a gentle pat. Sidney looked at me, wiped the sweat (?) out of his eyes with the back of his hand, took a deep breath, and drove us ever deeper into the forest primeval . . . the treasure that is Tara, with the treasure that is Anna sitting between the two of us.

Little girls know how to make things right.

Sacred Places

The sea was murmuring in the stillness of the Caribbean morning. I could hear it down beyond the palms to the east, low pitched, resonating, and restless, as I stood on the balcony of my residence, sipping on a cup of coffee, watching the first grey streaks of dawn on the eastern horizon. It had rained during the night. The air was fresh but also soft and thick. Back in the kitchen I could hear my friend Eric Dibble stirring around, finding his cup and pouring himself his first coffee of the day.

We were on an assignment, conducting research in Humacao Natural Reserve down along the east coast of Puerto Rico. Our mission was to study the fisheries in a series of small lagoons just down the road from where we were staying, and to determine how the fish and the people who exploited them were influenced by the different environments in the lagoons. We had two graduate students, Orlando Ferrer from Venezuela and Kirk Rundle from Virginia, working with us. While we traveled back and forth between Mississippi State

University and Puerto Rico, Orlando and Kirk maintained residence near the reserve. They'd been in Puerto Rico working on the project for nearly a year. Eric and I came down every three or four months, just to make sure everything was working smoothly.

The lagoons are small by continental standards but large from the perspective of island people, ranging in size from about five acres up to about four hundred acres. Along the series, lagoons closer to the sea were turbid and pretty salty. But by the time you get to the end of the series, the water clears and becomes more brackish. Over the months we'd learned that the last lagoon in the series, perhaps the most remote one from a fisheries perspective, was full of little tarpon ranging in size up to about ten pounds.

Today was Sunday and we would not be working. Rather, Eric and I planned to fish for those tarpon. Our students had left a boat for us by the lagoon and had warned us that, from their experience, it was best to fish as early as possible in the morning. They said that once the sun rose, the tarpon got real spooky and hard to catch.

Eric and I both poured ourselves another cup of coffee, stretched a little, and made our way down the stairway to the parking lot where our rental car was stationed. There were hardly any other vehicles on the road to the reserve's entrance. We had plenty of time and so just plugged along, swerving occasionally to dodge a chuckhole in the pavement or an occasional chicken. We made it to the gate in about ten minutes, parked our car, and started the twenty-minute walk along the trail leading to the last lagoon and our boat.

A few birds were calling softly, sleepily. A mongoose slipped out of the bushes on one side of the trail ahead of us, stopped, stared at us with its beady, expressionless eyes, then darted into a tangle of vines on the other side of the trail, on his way to conduct his daily business of being a foreign invader, robbing nests of ground-dwelling birds and eating the local lizards. In the shadows a heron stood motionless, waiting for a fish to drift near enough to be speared and eaten. To the east were the faint beginnings of what seemed destined to be a spectacular sunrise.

We located the boat, loaded our fishing tackle and ourselves, and shoved off into the clear water of the lagoon. In the shallows ahead of us we could see swirls made by tarpon as they bushwhacked tilapia. The submerged vegetation was predominately hydrilla and was matted just below the water's surface in large clumps. We quietly paddled the boat through natural channels between the vegetation mats, from one open pocket to the next.

We decided that it would be best for us to take turns fishing and paddling the boat. Eric was up first for fishing. The spinning rod that we used was not a very expensive piece of equipment, but it was solid and built to give an angler a bit of backbone when setting the hook. The open-faced reel was filled with twenty-pound test line. Our students, speaking from experience, had recommended that we fish with metal spoons equipped with treble hooks. These lures had plenty of flash and were heavy enough that we could cast pretty far ahead of the boat. This last aspect was important because the tarpon were pretty spooky. They'd shut down completely if they saw or heard the boat. We had to be careful, stalking them almost as hunters rather than as fishermen.

Eric cast at several of the tarpon before he got a strike. The tarpon rushed the silver spoon, smashed into it, and immediately went airborne, shaking its head a couple of times. The last shake threw the lure back almost to our boat.

A few casts later and Eric was into another fish. This time Eric came back very hard with the rod a couple of times in an attempt to drive the point of the hook deeply into the tarpon's boney mouth. The tarpon jumped, ran a few yards, and then jumped again. Then it did a tailwalk across the surface of the lagoon. The hook held tightly as Eric fought the fish to the boat. Once the fish was at the boat, he carefully unhooked it, held it up for a photograph, then gently released it back into the lagoon, exhausted but swimming upright—a good sign that it would recover from its fight.

Then it was my turn. Eric handed the rod and reel to me and I gave him the paddle. Rather than sitting on one of the boat seats to fish, I decided to stand on the front seat to get a higher perspective. I wanted to be able to see the fish out farther away from the boat so that we could plan our stalks.

It wasn't long, perhaps a minute or two, before I saw my first fish. I pointed out the location to Eric and coached him along for a while until he also could see the tarpon. It was a pretty good fish, at least as large as the one Eric had landed. I refrained from casting as we moved closer. I figured that extra casting would alert the fish.

Slowly, ever so slowly, we approached the fish. It was still harassing the tilapia near a cluster of cattails. When I thought I was within casting distance I motioned to Eric to let the boat drift. The glide took us a few feet closer. I reeled the lure up to about ten inches from the end of the rod, moved the rod back over my shoulders, looked down at my fingertip to be sure that the line was on the crease under my knuckle, then let her rip.

The spoon sailed in a perfect arc, hitting the water about six feet in front of the fish. There was a rush in the shallow water, and almost immediately the fish was on. I jerked back hard, and the fish flew into the air. It landed on its side, and when it was back in the water, I jerked hard again, and then again, hoping to secure the hook in the fish's mouth.

The tarpon went berserk, jumping and twisting and rushing around the opening among the vegetation. Eric was whooping and I reeled with clinched teeth. There was power in this fish, more power than I'd anticipated. After the first few wild moves, it decided to take command of the situation and bore down on a tangle of old willow branches. If it made it to the branches that would

be the end. The line would tangle, the hook would probably foul on a branch, and the fish would break off.

The drag on the reel screamed. The rod bucked
and bowed. I leaned back, harder and harder, and then,
as if by magic, the fish turned, but I realized I was in
real trouble because the fish was coming straight back
toward me. I reeled as fast as I could to keep the hook
under tension as the fish charged back toward the boat.
Somehow I was able to keep up. Then the fish saw the
boat and spun around to go back toward the clearing.
But by this time the fight was almost out of him and I
was in control, or so I thought anyway. The fish darted
a little to the left, then to the right, and I played him
steadily, gaining line all the while.

I thought the fight was over when the fish was
about fifteen feet from the boat. Suddenly, the water
went wild again, and the fish was back in the air, throwing spray all over Eric and me. I held tight and so did the
hook. After another short run and a bit of bulldog head
thrashing under the water, the fish gave up and let me
bring it to the boat.

It was a gorgeous thing to see as it lay in the water
beside the boat on its side, gill covers heaving, eyes
directed at me, silver scales shimmering in the water.
We estimated its weight at about twelve pounds as I
lifted it from the water. Eric took a couple of pictures,
and then I put the fish back into the water. I held onto
it, moving it back and forth and from side to side, helping it restore its respiration and balance. Finally, it was
able to stay upright without me holding it, and I noticed

that its gill covers were moving with a steady rhythm. I backed my hands away from the fish and watched as it drifted back into the shadows that lay alongside one of the vegetation mats.

Just then the sun rose above the palms and a shaft of light shot across the lagoon. But the water remained still, without so much as a ripple on the surface. We continued fishing for another thirty minutes or so, but it was all over, just as our students had said that it would be. There were no more swirls in the shallows, no more slashing runs near the edges of weed beds. The tarpon were finished for the day, and so was our fishing.

We paddled over to a small wooden dock near the spot where we'd launched our boat. We tied the boat to the dock; then, after gathering our gear, we started back along the trail that led to where we'd parked our car near the refuge's headquarters building. Along the way we met a few other people who had come to the refuge for a morning of fishing. Most were trying to catch tilapia and snook. A young couple and their little boy were handlining for blue crabs.

A little farther down the trail we met an old man who was casting from a wooden pier. He had a thermos of hot coffee and offered us a cup. We accepted his offer. Little was said as we sat in the shadows, sipping the coffee and watching the old man fish. Lizards rustled in the dry leaves around the trees. A couple of ducks circled over the area and landed on the far end of the lagoon. The sun gained strength, and the heat of a tropical day wrapped itself around us. Patiently the old man cast again and again toward a deep shadowy spot under a large tree. I began to wonder if he was in some sort of trance and did not realize that every cast he made was to the exact same spot. Then suddenly the water boiled under the tree, the old man's fishing rod arched, and a silvery fish flew into the air, shaking its head and throwing spray all around.

We watched as the old man skillfully worked the fish to the shore. The tarpon was about the same size as the ones we'd caught earlier. Although many people do not consider tarpon a food fish, we'd noted in our studies of the lagoons that captured tarpon usually ended up on a stringer and were taken home for dinner. But the old man had a different perspective. Once he had the fish in hand, he gently unhooked it, held it up so that we could get a good look at it, and then carefully slid it back into the water, whispering something, as if he and the fish were old friends sharing a secret.

I suspected that this fish probably had been caught by this old man before and perhaps many times. I mentioned to him that our studies showed that there were many more tarpon in the next lagoon in the series. But he just looked at me, smiled, and said that this place was his spot and that there were enough fish here for him. He didn't need to go to another place.

I understood just what he meant because I too have my special places. I suspect that you also have them. Most sportsmen do. Just like the old man who fished in that lagoon, I too cast into the same "pools" time and time again, allowing my hooks to sink ever deeper. They are the places where I go to reconnect with the earth, God, and myself: a tiny patch of woods along the edge of my pastures where fox squirrels crash in the branches on still October mornings; a small creek not far from the small city where I live in Mississippi (but apparently known only to me as a fishing creek) where beautiful longear sunfish and tough little spotted bass lurk in clear pools; a woodland pond on my farm where wild ducks rush in on January sunrises to land at my feet; a clearing way back in my farm's quiet corner where deer drift from the shadows as twilight settles on the land.

I could and occasionally do go to other places, places where there are more fish to catch and more or bigger game to shoot. I've traveled far as a hunter and fisherman and have had grand adventure and tremendous success on these journeys. But I've found that the finest of all journeys tend to be those in deeper realms, of connection, of reflection, where I am among friends: my pond at dawn as bluegill suck at the water's surface; the gnarled old post oak that stands sentinel as a wild turkey scratches for acorns beneath my tree stand; the brush pile by the ancient sycamore where there is always a chickadee, a wren, and, during winter, usually a swamp rabbit; the patch of honeysuckle down by my creek where cardinals splash red on somber winter days; a dark wet swampy corner down deep in my woods where salamanders and spirits lurk . . . all places that call my name.

When I go to these familiar places there is a deep stirring within me. When I'm with them, surrounded by them, part of them, I breathe somehow deeper the vapors that drift from nature, become entranced, casting again and again into the spiritual pool that swirls with life. I am stilled, transcending beyond thought, beyond emotion, beyond individual being. I am merged into ethereal energy that brings all life into communion. The gun or the rod that I carry becomes an extension of me. The hunting and the fishing in these special places become sacraments, reconnections to the oversoul of all creation.

I looked at the old man fishing in the lagoon and saw myself. He looked at me, smiled, and began casting again. Eric and I nodded to the old man, thanked him for the coffee, and moved on down the trail, without talking, but both knowing that we'd just been guests in another man's sacred space.

Sirens' Call

The night is deep and the water dark. In the distance lights twinkle from the oil rigs like so many Christmas trees. The ship pitches and rolls as it moves with a rumble across the sea. Standing against the railing I am mesmerized by the white foam breaking along the waves from our bow wake. My thoughts drift and hold on to nothing in particular. The air is thick, but out here on the stern deck it is fresh. Inside the ship the smell of fish and diesel and cooking mingle to form an essence known only to the world of fishermen.

"Twenty years on this ship," I thought to myself, "twenty years of dragging nets across the bottom of the Gulf of Mexico, and the only thing that's changed is the color of my beard and the speed at which I go up and down the steep stairs between the decks."

I began my affair with this ship, the NOAA Research Vessel Oregon II, back when I was a graduate student doing my doctoral work at Auburn University. I was studying river fisheries but was interested in ichthyology, so one of the professors arranged the venture for me. That first trip was like no trip since. We traveled far, out to the edge of the continental shelf, in order to sample deep-water fish and shrimp. We were out for over three weeks, and during that time I developed sea legs and found friends. My berth on that first trip was down on the lower deck, in the forward compartment, first "stateroom" on the left. It was a cramped little room with bunk beds, a sink, and places to store your gear—nothing more. But nothing more was needed.

I could hear the sea crashing against the hull down there when I went to bed. It seemed to be sending a message to me, telling me that the only thing between me and disaster, perhaps even death, was that thin steel hull. But back then I didn't think too much about that sort of thing. I was too full of spit and vinegar and deep in the realms of adventuring. For some reason over the course of the years I was never assigned that berth again, until this trip. This time, I paid attention to the message from the sea as it spoke through that hull. Over the years listening to the earth's voices has become easier. Perhaps it is because life has become more precious with time.

I have maintained a very simple mission when at sea. I'm at sea just to be here. Most of the time I bring students with me. Sometimes (rarely) I try to give fisheries lectures. But the students tend to be distracted, particularly those who are for the first time experiencing life on a ship. It is best just to leave them alone. They will learn things out here that no lecture will ever provide.

I ramble and drift through the days. Even though thirty people may be on board this 180-foot-long ship, I can find privacy. A corner on the deck, or a spot in a laboratory, or a seat in the galley becomes sacred space, respected by others. The word "respect" is really central to life on the ship. Without it, life could become very rough and dirty out here. We all live so close together, constantly encountering each other. Smiles aren't required but they are common. There's a discipline to it. It is sort of a survival technique.

Each evening at 11:30 p.m. I'm awakened by one of the crew. My watch begins at midnight and I'm given thirty minutes to get myself collected and up to the fish processing laboratory near the stern deck. I crawl out of my bunk and instinctively hold onto the edge of the bed and sink to keep my balance as the ship rolls. I slip into my work clothes and climb the steps up to the main deck, passing the galley on the way. The smell of fresh coffee is strong and inviting. But first I want to look at the lab to see if there are any fish onboard, and at the rigging on the stern deck to see if there is a net out fishing. Only then do I go back to the galley for coffee. Typically there will be other ship's crew and students on my watch gathered there, munching on something, watching the news on satellite TV, trying to get themselves collected and ready for eight hours of work.

I pour myself a cup of coffee, greet the folks in the galley, then slip out again to the stern deck to breathe the fresh air, look at the stars, and reflect on the reality of being out here working in the ocean. It is pretty awesome and this ship seems so small. I've been in storms out here on this ship. I've been thrown from bed, dishes have crashed in the galley, walking was virtually impossible. The ship shudders, hesitates, grinds sometimes at air when the stern is lifted, then catches and plows on. Water washes across the decks, and we hunker down inside our tiny world of steel. It is our spaceship, our life support system. But this night it is fairly calm, just gentle swells and hardly any wind . . . a sailor's delight.

Although I've enjoyed my times at sea, and even though I've been out here for two decades, I have intentionally maintained a sort of barrier between my professional identity and the inner circle of marine fisheries. It has been enough for me to reconnect just a little, to remember the names of some of the fish, to gaze at horizons, sunsets, sunrises, to talk with the crew and encourage students who seem especially interested in the work. But this trip was different. This trip had a mission. I was being challenged to make a decision that could bring major changes to the fisheries program I direct at Mississippi State University. I had time to reflect—eight days this trip—to think, to connect, to test the waters, to listen to the winds of my soul and perhaps pay attention to the messages from the sea.

During a fisheries conference held in Canada a few months prior to this trip I'd been approached by one of the senior staff administrators of the National Marine Fisheries Service Laboratory down in Pascagoula, Mississippi, with regard to ramping up my involvement in their program. The opportunity for moving into the dimension of marine fisheries research, with funded projects, graduate students, and logistical support was outlined to me. I was no stranger to this kind of work, having recently conducted tarpon and snook studies down in the Caribbean that resulted in an M.S. thesis and a Ph.D. dissertation. That had been fun. But I really never considered it as a prelude to something more, because my professional reputation was centered around inland fisheries, and particularly those associated with floodplain river ecosystems. I'd been working with rivers for more than twenty years. To move into marine fisheries would require redefining a lot of who I am and what I do.

The rivers speak to me. I can shut my eyes and hear their voices. I am deeply connected to their rhythms. I understand beyond words their processes. I can sense their forces, and I know where the fish are and how and why they do what they do. I relate to the crusty folks who fish the rivers, the recreational anglers, the commercial fishermen, and those who fish for subsistence purposes. They are my people. I am one of them. There certainly are still unanswered questions for me as a scientist working with rivers, but as a poet, as a naturalist, my connection with rivers is fully engaged. Could I, should I, begin a similar journey with the sea?

As I stood out there on the stern deck the sky lightened in the east and the sea turned from black to grey to green. I sipped on my coffee. The ship's crew stirred to ready the nets for the dawn trawl. I knew their moves well. I watched as they positioned the otter boards and checked the lazy line, the tickler chain, and codend. With a word from the bridge the net slipped over the railing, into the sea, and the boards were lowered. When they touched the water they bucked, then caught, then spread, swinging wider and wider until constrained at the maximum distance allowed by the net. The man on the winch continued to lower the rig until the proper depth was achieved, then locked it down. Most of our trawls were thirty minutes. I had time to get another cup of coffee before the net would be retrieved.

Back in the galley a fresh pot of coffee was waiting, and the cook was busy getting breakfast ready. The smell of bacon hung heavy in the air. The news on the TV was about war and tragedy and politics. I quickly poured my coffee and returned outside. I needed a different focus for this day. And so I turned to the sea and within it, upon it, found a realm of separate peace.

I looked out across the water, and in the distance there were two shrimp boats. I knew that the people on those boats were hard-working folks, trying to make a living from the sea. If things didn't go right, they wouldn't be able to pay their bills, they wouldn't be able to take care of their kids, they'd have a tough time with mortgages, insurance, groceries. They lived on an edge. And in their work, in their lives, were the decisions made by fisheries professionals and politicians coached by them. If the fisheries work wasn't done and done well, they suffered. They too were my people.

The sea that hammered at the hull by my bunk spoke again to me, but this time out in the open. I listened hard. The winch began to whine and grind, bringing in the trawl. I broke into the rhythm of fishing, donned my hard hat, life jacket, and rubberized overalls, and prepared to receive the catch. The crewman on the deck with me reached out with a long aluminum pole with a hook to grab the lazy line. The pole swung across the deck, and he grabbed the line with his hand, uncoupling it from the boards and onto another line attached to a different winch. Bracing himself, he ran the line through a large hook on the railing and the winch started hauling the net onboard. A few wraps around the codend with another rope, a swing with the boom handling the cable, and the catch was onboard.

I quickly moved to where the codend hung swinging over the catch area on the stern. Positioning large baskets under the net I worked with the crewman as he loosened the tie rope around the codend and let the catch out.

And what a marvelous catch it was! Shrimp, crabs, fish of all kinds, even a couple of small sharks, tumbled into the baskets. For a fisherman, for a fisheries biologist, it was like being eight years old and turning on the lights early on a Christmas morning, with all the glories of Santa (or God—at that age I had them mixed together) spread out before you. I could hardly take my eyes off that catch, it was so beautiful. And yet I'd seen many similar and many better catches before. Why the difference? Why did this particular catch touch me this way?

And then the sea spoke to me again, and I looked up from the catch and saw those two shrimp boats moving out and away from us. And a message swelled up from my heart and I understood.

There was something deeper than a place, something deeper than a way, something deeper, in a spiritual sense, than a river. Deeper than all waters was the *connection* humankind has to those waters, river, ocean, lake, or lagoon . . . we cast our nets and join in eternal drama. This was a message I'd heard before, back when I'd left seminary and the pastoral ministry and moved onto another path, a path awash with light showing the way, the path of "feeding His sheep," to become a fisheries biologist.

The siren song did not come from mermaids but rather from a source more similar to my childhood concept of Santa. There is strength and assurance in that call. It gives me peace, gives me energy, and, when I closed my eyes and stood there listening to the rumble of the ship, feeling the sway under my feet, smelling the salt air laced with the odor of fish on the deck, I had a vision of the sea's fisheries and the people who depend on them . . . and I saw a river feeding them all.

Before the Five

Flames dance in the fireplace on this February night, thin yellow-blue wisps reaching upward from the split wood, orange coals shimmering below. I am drawn into the flames and through them, beyond them, onward into a deep current, into a realm where thought and soul and dreams and memories and longings swirl. There is a call, really more of a cry, and it penetrates all that I am, and grips me.

I am of the wild. There's a blade in my soul that cuts and slashes until I'm outside of all bounds, until I'm beyond the entanglements of all bonds, until I'm enveloped by that beautiful sweet loneliness of the trackless way. It is not something that can be shaken. It will not be stilled. The wild draws me, commands me, consumes me. All I have to do is relax for a moment, let down my guard, and I am lost in it.

The flames before me send me soaring through time and space until I am back in the lonely places. I am in an Ozark valley full of hush as twilight and chill drift from the winter hills. Eternity brushes my senses and surrounds my heart. The trees on the skyline are a thousand sentinels. The chime of the stream on ice just beyond the camp is as if from a cathedral, reminding me that just like the day, just like the stream, I too am passing. There is no sadness in this. It is the way of all things. Peace settles on the camp . . . on my heart . . . and I draw close to the fire, smoke rising straight into a windless, crisp, and brittle night, taking the essence of earth into the heavens. And the glory of the night sky is accented by the echoes of owl calls bouncing from the cliffs. There is no other companion with me. I do not need talk beyond nature's messages. I do not need companionship except for the dark hills.

Rising in restlessness a little while ago, I drifted from my living room and went outside to embrace the night air. While I was out there, I got another log from the pile beside my door for the fireplace. The first rush of new flame, that sudden surge that occurred after I put that piece of wood on the flickering embers, now has settled and mellowed. So have I . . . just a little.

I am surrounded by the embers of family and home, one son and my daughter here in the living room with me, each drifting into their own dreamtime, exploring the world within them and beyond, reading books and searching the computer networks. My other son is with a youth group at church, off alone with the family car, a young man proven responsible and trustworthy countless times. My wife drifts in to join us in the living room and selects music for the evening, as graceful as a whitetail doe in her movements, as elegant as a wood duck hen gliding across my woodland pond, and as haunting and mysterious as the call of snow geese in a boundlessly deep winter sky. How can she know, how can she understand the true power of those images, what they mean to me, and how I see their essence reflected in her? There is really no way for treasure to know treasure.

The log shifted on the coals a few moments ago, and new flames sprang from its sides. My flames also shifted inside of me, and now I hear the rushing of runners on a frozen river. The dogs ahead of me pull in rhythm, a steady pace, fast and sure, with the wind whipping past us and only a lone raven overhead telling us that there is life in the white world around us. We go just to be going, there is no ultimate goal, only to be back some-time before the aurora ripples through the heavens. But even if it catches us still on that frozen river, it is of no matter. It is never really dark on a winter's night in Alaska. The snow catches starlight and moonlight and makes night travel magical. I stand on the sleigh's run-ners, my parka, wool pants, mittens, and knit hat keep-ing me warm, except for my eyes (which are cold and watering) and my cheeks (which are stiff). Ten miles, twenty miles, thirty miles . . . on and on, then from the cast of the golden late afternoon light, I know it is time to turn. But I make the turn too quickly, don't apply the break deeply enough in the snow, and the sled tumbles. The dogs stop as I retrieve myself, brushing off the snow. I right the sled and make sure the harnesses are straight and secure. Then we're off again. A moose cuts across the river in front of us and plunges into the spruce forest that stretches beyond the shoreline. The dogs surge forward. I shout at them and press hard on the sled's break. They strain, but I'm in control. They know this and settle back into the whisper and rush of wind and runners, occasionally biting a chunk of snow to help quench their thirst.

How quickly the fire consumes the logs I put on it. How quickly a life consumes the chapters of its pilgrimage. I left my beloved Ozark hills, and also Alaska, one after another, over twenty years ago, but still they haunt me. There are embers that seem never to cool, and all I have to do is put another log on the fire to get it all stirred up again. I do that knowing that it will hurt, time and again. Tonight the log I put on the fire was an Alaskan story written by Jack London. I knew when I picked it up that I was playing with fire, literally.

I left the lands that own my heart for good reason, but the call to be there, to be again wild, to be again of the wild, surges and churns and screams and throws itself all across my mind, pulling me from any hope of contentment and peace, plaguing me incessantly with images and memories and dreams. I'm forever in the hills, looking down at a green ribbon of river from some perch on a high rocky cliff and seeing an eagle soaring far below me. I'm forever upon Ozark streams with my canoe, churning my way through the rapids, forever watching a red fox hunt in the stillness of a late winter afternoon and then sucking on my knuckle, squeaking like a woodland mouse, and having that fox come straight to me; I'm forever in the frozen mountains of Alaska, looking out across glaciers; I'm forever smelling the dank sweetness of a freshly killed bear, hearing the rasping, rattling call of sandhill cranes in the marshes and out on the tidal flats; I'm captured by the majesty of a bull moose in the alders and the poetry of Dall sheep on green slopes. The pastel pink, ever so faint, on the sides of a grayling fresh from an icy creek is the essence of an Alaskan sunrise captured in miniature. The steam spouting from the nostrils of a caribou as it trots at full speed across tundra and out of your life forever is the essence of wilderness.

And yet I've stayed here in Mississippi all these years. Why? It didn't have to be this way . . . or did it? I didn't want to leave the Ozarks. I didn't want to leave Alaska. But something pulled me from these lands so many years ago and put me here where there is another sort of wild, a wild on a different scale, within a different dimension. There was a mission here. There still is. So I stayed and a life has taken root. It isn't what I thought it would be, but then isn't that the way it is in wilderness? We move boldly and steadily into the unknown and adapt ourselves to that which we meet along the way.

The flames in my fireplace now speak a new message to me: "Get up and get us another stick of wood or else our coals will chill and so will your house." In obedience I stir from my spot in the living room and go back outside for the wood. I stand for a few minutes under the heavens. The night is still, calm, deep, full of mystery, and getting much colder. It snowed this morning—not much—but there was just the faintest hint of a wilder way, a wilder earth, a wilder spirit mixed in with it.

Taking a deep breath, I turn, come back into the house, and put the new log on the coals. The fire before me immediately jumps back into bright flame. And, primed by the magic of a winter's night, so does the one within me. I know that early tomorrow morning I'll be out in it all, running my trap line, crunching across a frozen pasture with frost sparkling in the starlight, probing the shadows of the woods and skirting the edges of my pond, connecting with wilderness before dawn.

I'm alone now before the fire. My family has gone to bed. I gaze long and deep at the flickering blaze. All is quiet except for the fire. I listen carefully. I can hear whispers from the flame, whispers from the other side. The fire is eternal.

Sacraments*

God of heaven and of earth, we gather together to celebrate the beauty and mysteries of the world around us and the spirit that swells within us as individuals and among us as a united people and dedicate ourselves anew to the purposes of working in wildlife conservation. We are awed by the processes through which your creation continues to evolve. We sense the flow of your energy through the ages. We are humbled by our roles as partners with you in this process, linking with nature, transcending self, dedicating life forces, even life itself, to ensure that future life can know your universe as we have been blessed to know it.

We meet you most powerfully in the cathedrals of the wild and lonely places: the forests, the fields, the wetlands, the rivers, the seas. You have adorned the cathedrals with sunrises, sunsets, clear winter skies, waterfalls, surf, and fireflies. Days spent outdoors are

*Invocation given to the Mississippi Wildlife Federation

sacraments. Our lives become in themselves prayers of the most powerful kind, prayers that echo through the ages and that become dimensions of immortality. The choirs of your cathedral sing their unending praise, each section blending movement into movement: the opening measures of a gobbler at sunrise, the whisper of wind in the pines, the melody of geese overhead, the bugle of hounds on the trail, the rush of a summer thunderstorm, the chorus of frogs at dusk, the crescendo of teal as they sweep low over decoys, the refrain of children playing and splashing in a stream.

We hear your messages. We pass the messages, our heritage, our history, along to others, in camps, Jeeps, boats, stands, blinds, backyards, and other quiet, powerful places in the wild known only to us. We are instructed by and tempered by earth forces beyond the realm of humankind's control. Through these lessons, and in humbleness, we sense how small we are, and how large the drama unfolding. We recognize that we are a part of nature, not apart from nature. And in this recognition we are truly blessed, for there are those who have yet to see this light. Give us patience as we reach out to these persons. Help us to understand their fears and insecurities. Bridge the chasms that separate us so that we can unite as we leave our footprints on the earth, footprints that reflect synchrony with the rhythms of the earth.

We leave your cathedrals energized, focused, renewed, and committed to standing firm, with solid resolve and vision. We are a people who care, but caring is not enough. We are called to action and charged with mission. We lift our collective voices to say that we will not allow the desecration of our sanctuaries and that we will not give up our sacraments.

And so we gather, perhaps as warriors, perhaps as guides, perhaps as compasses for our society, our civilization, asking for your direction, praying for your energy to renew *our* energies, and your spirit within us, so that we may be instruments of your peace, givers, not takers. Bind us together. Bond us together. Bless us. Help us to be a positive force in your universe. AMEN.